A QUAKER MISCELLANY
FOR
EDWARD H.MILLIGAN

A
Quaker Miscellany
for
Edward H. Milligan

Edited by David Blamires, Jeremy Greenwood and Alex Kerr

David Blamires, Manchester, 1985

Special edition for E.H.M.: ISBN 0 9510152 0 6
Ordinary edition: ISBN 0 9510152 1 4

Printed in Great Britain by
Headley Brothers Ltd, The Invicta Press, Ashford, Kent

Distributed by
FRIENDS BOOK CENTRE
Euston Road, London NW1 2BJ

CONTENTS

EDWARD H.MILLIGAN

What tense are we to write in? Past, present and future, but chiefly the present, even if we refer to things past. As Librarian of London Yearly Meeting at Friends House from 1957 to 1985 Edward Hyslop Milligan (to give him his full name for once) is known throughout the Society of Friends and beyond as deeply and extraordinarily knowledgeable on a myriad points of Quaker history and practice. This knowledge is never simply antiquarian, but always at the service of the present and, since the present is never still, given with a careful eye to the future. Ted is apt to speak of yearly meetings that took place a hundred years or more ago as if he himself had been present at them and witnessed their contributions from end to end. His gift for discerning the relevance of seemingly ancient debates to the issues of the immediate present and for making the past come newly alive cannot be matched. Many a yearly meeting or commit-tee document has been enriched by this rare capacity for sketching in the necessary historical background, grasping the present issue firmly and foreseeing the implications of possible paths of action. The continuities are important. The past feeds the present as surely as the present gives birth to the future.

Ted's wide-ranging knowledge of Quakerism has always been gener-ously placed at the disposal of all who have consulted him. His own personal contribution to Quaker historiography in terms of books and articles is not large, but his name is mentioned appreciatively in the forewords of scores of studies on Quaker topics or topics with Quaker ramifications. Everyone who has contributed to this book of essays writes out of gratitude for Ted's guidance and judgement. We are all conscious that on many points Ted knows more and better than we do. Blessed with a retentive and luxuriant memory and a sharp, catholic intellect, he has a zest for accuracy that is marvellously calm and unshowy.

The essays included in this book have a bias to the historical, as might be expected. They cover virtually every period of Quaker history in both Britain and Ireland and range widely in their subjects. That is as it should be. But it is also important to us that the book contains reflective and personal contributions that have to do with the present and the immediate past of the Society. Except for Tom Bodine's essay, which takes us across the Atlantic into American Quakerism, these latter contributions stem chiefly from colleagues and friends who have worked closely with Ted at Friends House in the national life of Friends. Much of Ted's energy and wisdom has centred on the life of London Yearly Meeting and will no doubt continue to do so even after he has left the staff of Friends House. Probably his most distinctive writing and that which he has most enjoyed has found its way into the official documents of the Yearly Meeting. Many a potentially dull or conventional report has been enlivened by his skill, his touches of humour and illustrative asides—above all a continuing delight in the tales of Beatrix Potter.

So, dear Ted, here is our book, our token of friendship and gratitude for your service as Librarian for the Religious Society of Friends in Great Britain. We hope that you will enjoy reading it and forgive the mistakes and misapprehensions which you would have gently corrected if you had been consulted. We hope too that many others will gain pleasure and instruction from what we have enjoyed putting together for you.

DAVID BLAMIRES   JEREMY GREENWOOD   ALEX KERR

'MY! HOW YOU'VE GROWN!'

by Chris Barber

This has remained for several generations the standard remark which older people, like great-aunts and uncles, address to children that they have not seen for a while. The context in which I best recall the expression was the Barber family party. This was no little party of Mum, Dad, the kids and a few relatives. This was a grand affair. 'Grand' is the right word, for in my day, the late 1920s and early thirties, it took place in the ballroom of the Grand Hotel in Sheffield. It had begun as an annual event when the descendants of James Henry Barber (1820-1902) were invited to his eldest daughter's home. It moved to the Grand Hotel when this became necessary to fit in the numbers. How many were there, I cannot guess, but descendants of James Henry Barber living in the Sheffield area numbered about fifty or sixty and some came from a distance like Brayshaws from Manchester. To a small boy it seemed huge. Children were organised in groups in the middle of the room and adults sat around the outside talking and gossiping, often, I think, studying the young and how they were coming on—'My! How he's grown!' and all that. There was no lack of talent for entertaining the children; some 'games' like the Family Coach and the Tramride were probably original; others like musical chairs were well-worn.

By no means all the family were Quakers. Quite a number of my father's generation had married non-Friends and had moved away to other churches. But Hartshead Meeting in Sheffield, to which we went faithfully during my boyhood (1925-37), contained a sprinkling of relatives among its members. Uncle (great) Ted, the humorous, story-telling, pipe-smoking uncle *par excellence* and Auntie May, equally good fun (she turned out later to have a secret vice that we knew not of at that time—she took snuff, of all things); a family of Doncaster cousins with boys about my age who sat opposite us; older female Doncaster cousins, one of whom could be guaranteed to chuck my sisters' chins and murmur 'these nice girls'; and a Priestman great-uncle who, it was vaguely hinted, had been rather off the responsible rails for much of life before returning to the fold.

It was quite a large meeting with a good number of younger Friends, some of whom would visit us on summer evenings to play tennis. But looking back, the key figures in a way were neither this younger element nor the relatives but a few of a rather different background. Later in life when I heard people argue that Friends were a set of middle-class intellectuals, I would counter by maintaining that I had been brought up in a largely working-class meeting. It was only true up to a point and, I now realise, an unusual case. The working-class element came from the Adult School activity. Men had come to Hartshead first to get education. I can remember more than once my father chatting to someone in the street or at Bramall Lane cricket ground and then telling me after that that was a man he had taught to read and write. The education led to attending meeting. And what good contributors these men were. When we were young, William Powell would tell us delightful stories for our benefit before we went below for Sunday School. Fred Tring produced what I, as a schoolboy, felt to be great thoughts. One always knew when he was about to minister as he crossed and re-crossed his legs two or three times in five minutes. And then when he stood, he invariably began with the words 'Whilst I've been sat 'ere . . .'. So at that time we had the security of family connections, the liveliness of some younger people and we listened to ministry of beautiful words with dropped aitches.

What of the customs of the meeting? As elsewhere, then and for many years, Friends would sometimes go down on their knees for vocal prayer and then we would all stand up. I actually enjoyed the chance of stretching my legs and was grateful to Auntie May—a regular kneeler. But I am not sure that it was custom elsewhere, as it was at Hartshead, for men to come into meeting actually wearing their hats—bowlers or sometimes trilbies. When they sat down they would take their hats off and put them under their seats. As my father explained, a meeting is not, as is a church, a house of God; there is no need to take your hat off when entering. It is when you settle for worship that you are in the presence of God. It had been a custom of practical value on one occasion when an elder found himself alone in the elders' gallery—yes, we used the first level up for the elders to sit—and he was some distance from the nearest Friend; he ended meeting by simply putting on his hat rather than by shaking hands. I do not recall that when meeting closed we were much given to shaking hands with our neighbours, let alone holding hands all round. Of course the women all wore hats. Dress was important. Sunday Best was the rule and the men would be wearing undoubtedly their Sunday suits. I remember my father being really quite angry with me when he once discovered in the meeting house yard before meeting that I had come in slippers, not walking shoes. I had let down the Sunday Best image. Along with Sunday Best went Lord's Day Observance. Our household, although devoted to sport, had no games on Sunday, unless it was word games like thinking of Bible characters beginning with a particular letter of the alphabet. Chess and draughts crept into Sunday at some stage but never cards. That makes life in the Barber family sound a bit dull, but far from it! We had lots of fun and laughter at home.

On the other hand I do not recall many touches of humour at meeting for worship or in preparative meeting (I never went to a monthly or quarterly meeting at that stage). There was one incident in preparative meeting that I do remember relishing at the time. A Friend—another Barber relative—announced that she so enjoyed and valued meetings for worship that she hoped we might extend the time from one hour to $1\frac{1}{4}$ hours each Sunday. There was obvious but silent consternation at this proposal but no one could think of a sound reason for keeping to the hour until, after a long silence, a large woman Friend at the back wearing a big navy-blue hat said, 'Well, in that case I wouldn't be 'ome in time to cook family dinner'. The Clerk took that as the feeling of the meeting and proceeded to next business.

In fact I think laughter has come to play an important part in our meetings in recent years. I love the ripples of laughter that spread across the large assembly of a yearly meeting. They seem to indicate a fellowship through common response, a sort of movement of the spirit. In monthly meetings too, a bit of humour seems to hold us together and help us along without detracting from our serious purpose. However, humorous interjections like that suffered by a well-known Friend, Edward H. Milligan, who was rhetorically asking what Friends would think if he was seen coming out of a public-house, when he was held up by a voice saying 'much more worried to see you going *in*, Ted', may be barred as bordering on heckling, which is not in right Quaker ordering. Funny stories in meeting for worship on Sunday may be a thing for the future but perhaps Reading Meeting, as in other things, was leading the way when a Friend, now an elder, managed to use in ministry a story of two nuns getting off a bus. One says, 'I thought those two men sitting next to us were rather unpleasant'. The other responds, 'Well, one of them was kind to animals. I distinctly heard him say he'd put his last shirt on a sick horse'. I doubt if that would have been risked in Hartshead Meeting in 1930.

We have seen so many changes in style and behaviour over a couple of generations. We men no longer walk into meeting in bowler hats; many of us do not even have hats. We no longer feel obliged to wear suits—or walking shoes. We do not use our elders' galleries, preferring to be all at one level and, if possible, round in a circle. We do not kneel to pray or stand when someone does. We are more likely to shake hands—or even hold hands—at the end of meeting. In our business meetings, we have tended to abandon full names in our minutes so that Christopher B. Barber has become Chris Barber, much to his pleasure in fact. Our First Day is Sunday; and our First Month is January. (That reminds me that I did enjoy a letter in *The Friend*, once, that suggested that as the planets of the solar system were named after heathen gods, Friends should refer to Mercury as First Planet, Venus as Second Planet and so on.) Humour and laughter have become more acceptable. The distinction between birthright and convinced Friends seems to be being forgotten and Quaker families predominate less in our meetings.

Even if I allow for the fact that much of the change in the Society of Friends over this period merely reflects the changes in society in general, I think I could don the mantle of one of my great-aunts and say to the Society, 'My! How you've changed!'.

Can I, I wonder, say 'My! How you've grown!'?

The Society has not grown numerically, which means that any suggestion that there has been growth, implies a growth in spiritual quality or in influence, perhaps. Any assessment is bound to be subjective but there are some things one can say when reviewing the changes.

As Quakers we have to discard some of the trappings and prejudices of the world around us but still be *of* this world, in which we have faith—as being God's world. We have to dissociate ourselves from many of the attitudes and actions of people around us and yet be *of* the people, in whom we have faith—as having that of God.

This is a sort of art in which we are guided by the spirit and by our understanding of Quaker insights and in which we are often influenced by our fellow members. It is the art of taking up the right stance or posture. Our stance has to be one which is in the world and open to the world but at the same time open to being moved of the spirit and genuinely seeking guidance from our understanding of the essence of the Christian message.

I think we may be weaker than we were in our understanding of the Christian message; certainly, we seem to be less well-versed in our Bible. But I do think we have grown better or stronger in our ability to take the right stance. Of course, we are all different in personality, ability and background and we shall each take up our own position, but collectively, as

4

a Society, I think we are more in the world, more open to it and, probably, more open to the spirit.

More *in* the world because we have let out some of our Quaker jargon and peculiarities of the past (First Month) and substituted terms and customs of the wider world (January). We have let out the need to be respectable (the Sunday suit) and let in a breath of naturalness and informality.

More open to the world because we have let in more laughter and let out some gravity and pompousness. We have been more accepting of people, both outside the Society and within; our changed attitude to homosexuals is a case in point.

Probably more open to the spirit because such openness involves being less cluttered with unimportant customs and freer of guilt about propriety and respectability. And probably more open to the spirit because such openness is helped by removing barriers to fellowship and improving corporate communication. The abandonment of those elders' galleries, the sitting more often in a circle, more shaking hands, less hierarchy, the forgetting of distinctions between birthright and convinced Friends and the reduced distinction between members and attenders; all these indicate a stronger and more egalitarian fellowship. And don't we love getting together, as witness our record Yearly Meeting attendances? All these things lead me to feel that we are more open to the spirit, at least to the extent that it is mediated to us through our fellows.

More in the world, more open to the world and probably more open to the spirit. My! Maybe we've grown after all!

JOSEPH SHERWOOD, QUAKER ATTORNEY AND NOTARY c.1734-73

by Melanie Barber

Inclosed your Grace will receive a Petition which has been addressed to me as Master of the Facultyes by one of the People called Quakers, who therein desires to be made a Publick Notary and has annexed to it several Extracts from Acts of Parliament in relation to some indulgences granted by the Legislature to persons of this persuasion. If the desired Faculty had been to exercise The Office of a Notary in any of the Plantations, I should not have hesitated about it. But, as upon Inquiry & upon a Search of the Files of Paper & Book in the Faculty Office, I don't find that any Quaker has before this made any such application, It must be considered as a new case. It is usual to say in these sort of Petitions to the Master of the Facultyes that the Petitioner is a person well affected to the Government in *Church* & State, and How far this provision restrains it to a person of the Established Church, I could wish to submit to your Grace; As also whether there is or is not any Implication to be drawn from the Statute which allows a Quaker to be an Attorney or Sollicitor in favour of his being a Publick Notary, as I am indeed sorry to be forced to say, that this seemingly peaceable & inoffensive Sect are very apt to be very clamourous about Tythes, Church Powers, and other Ecclesiastical matters.[1]

So wrote Francis Topham, Master of the Faculties, to Thomas Secker, Archbishop of Canterbury, on receiving the application of Joseph Sherwood to be admitted a notary public in March 1760. This letter is the first in a correspondence[2] that is of interest not only for the light that it sheds, in an unguarded moment, on the Church's attitude towards Quakers, but also for the attention it focuses on an otherwise little known Friend whose brief career illustrates the workings of the Society at many different levels.

At the time of his application, Joseph Sherwood of Austin Friars in the parish of St Peter le Poer, London, was a young attorney-at-law, aged between twenty-five and twenty-six. He had been admitted an attorney in the Court of King's Bench in Michaelmas term 1754 and a solicitor in the Court of Chancery in February 1755.[3] In August 1759, he had been chosen by the General Assembly of Rhode Island as agent for the colony 'at the court of Great Britain'[4] in succession to Richard Partridge, a London Quaker merchant, who had held this position since 1715. A few days before his death in March 1759, Partridge had written to the Governor of Rhode Island strongly recommending the appointment of Sherwood whom he had used for agency business and had 'found him Capable and Attentive to Business and carefull to Discharge his Duty with Fidelity and application'.[5] As proof of his confidence in his abilities, he had appointed him one of his executors. It was Sherwood's appointment as a colonial agent that prompted his application for admission as a notary.

The right of appointing notaries was conferred on the Archbishop of Canterbury by Peter's Pence Act, 1534. The act set up the Faculty Office and it was through the Master of the Faculties that the Archbishop exercised the dispensing and licensing powers previously enjoyed by the Pope, such as the issue of dispensations for clergy to hold in plurality, marriage licences, degrees and the admission of notaries. Applicants for appointment as notaries were required to provide certificates signed by practising notaries, testifying to their character, integrity, competency and professional expertise. Most certificates stated that the applicant was 'conformable to the Church of England'. However the appointment was not restricted to Anglicans and, in the case of Jews, for instance, the phrase was omitted. The appointment of a Quaker notary was not unprecedented, but the Master of the Faculties did not discover the precedent until late in his negotiations. Daniel Maude of Bermondsey, factor, aged fifty, had applied to a previous Master of the Faculties in 1732 and had been admitted within a week of applying—it is doubtful that it was considered necessary to consult the Archbishop, William Wake.[6]

By the time of Sherwood's application, Daniel Maude had been dead about twenty years and the precedent had been temporarily forgotten. That the Master of the Faculties saw fit to consult Archbishop Secker in 1760 is possibly indicative of a change of attitude to Quakers during the primacy of Secker. Secker's reply to Topham's letter was cautious. He observed that there were Jewish notaries though 'There may indeed be greater need that some Jews should be public Notaries than that any Quakers should'. He presumed that the Master was not bound to admit anyone; nor would he choose 'to have a Quaker made, unless refusing him would raise a Clamour, for they are extremely apt to be perverse in every thing. Yet I know not that this Office will give them any opportunities of being so'. The Archbishop questioned the nature of the appointment: how far was it an ecclesiastical office within the meaning of the 1604 Canons whereby the recipient would have been required to subscribe to the Thirty-Nine Articles? How far could it be described as a civil office within the terms of the Test Act, under which those who did not receive the sacrament in the Church of England were disqualified from holding office? He wondered whether the oath to execute the office of notary faithfully was prescribed by statute or custom and, depending on the answer to this, whether the substitution of affirmation provided for in the 1722 Affirmation Act in all cases where an oath was required by statute was applicable. Having raised these queries, Secker went some way to answering them, but admitted apologetically:' I only suggest you see, what occurs to me, without giving any determinate Opinion'. He concluded by advising Topham to confer with 'the Gentlemen of the Commons' (the ecclesiastical lawyers of Doctors Commons), and play for time: 'excuse yourself in the meanwhile to the Petitioner on account of your Indisposition'[7] (he was indeed suffering from a severe attack of gout).

The Master of the Faculties lost little time in answering the points which he felt were 'matters of great importance, very proper and indeed highly necessary on this occasion to be taken into consideration'. He was guarded in his attempts to define the nature of the office of notary. He doubted that it could be defined as a civil office within the terms of the Test Act; equally he was inclined to deny that it was an ecclesiastical office within the meaning of the 1604 Canons. It was, he thought, 'of a mixed nature, sometimes employed in Civil, sometimes employed in Ecclesiastical Matters'. In answer to the question about his right to refuse admission, he looked at the variety of faculties or grants issued by the Faculty Office and made a distinction between those he considered to be 'matter of right' and others which were merely 'matter of favour'. In the former category, he placed 'all Faculties, Licences, & dispensations, as the Subjects of this Realm were wont & accustomed to receive of the See of Rome'. These could not legally or safely be denied if the candidate were otherwise duly qualified. On the other hand, where they were considered to be mere acts of grace and favour such as faculties for degrees in arts and science (Lambeth degrees), 'These being matter of mere favour & distinction and only to be conferred for the sake of publick utility, as an Encouragement to Learning & as a Reward thereof . . . the person conferring them is the sole & absolute judge without controul or appeal'. Having stated this distinction, he was still not entirely convinced of his obligation to admit a Quaker, though he indicated that every Jew who applied to be a notary was admitted. He was, however, apprehensive that 'refusing this or any other Quaker would be productive of much clamour which it most probably would be spread & propagated with all that Art & Industry which they have too much practised on some other occasions'. He feared that Friends would be justified in pointing out that important contracts and commissions were already transmitted to their agents here, and only required notarial attestation. If the same person were both agent/factor and notary, it would certainly help to expedite business sent from abroad. Nevertheless, he thought it advisable to consult other lawyers.[8]

The lawyers confirmed that it would be improper to refuse a Quaker what was constantly granted to a Jew. But Sherwood's appointment as agent for Rhode Island and his consequent involvement in commercial and mercantile negotiations clinched the case in his favour, for Topham wrote: 'The Circumstance of the Factorage & Commissions from Abroad give indeed further weight to this application'. To show the importance he attached to this, he proposed that Sherwood should provide a second certificate from 'merchants of eminence' who could not only testify to his skills but also to 'the convenience and propriety of his being made a notary';[9] this was in addition to the common certificate from notaries already supplied.

The wording of the two certificates was very similar. Both certified him to be 'a person of Sober Life and Conversation and well affected to his Majesty King George the Second and the Present Administration . . ., of known probity and well skilled in affairs of Notarial Concern', and therefore fitly qualified to be created a notary public.[10] But the signatories of the second were merchants and bankers; the latter were two leading Quaker firms of bankers: Henton Brown, who signed for himself and his son James (it was this London banker who is believed to have entertained Archbishop Herring on his daughter's marriage),[11] and Smith, Wright and Gray, bankers on Lombard Street, whom the astute Quaker diarist, James Jenkins, gave as an example of 'the surlies' whose crusty mode of conduct had at times brought them in for criticism.[12] On receipt of the certificate, Sherwood made the necessary affirmation (oaths of supremacy, allegiance, and of office were normally required), and he was admitted, 8 May 1760,[13] just over two months after his application.

What, one may well ask, is the significance of this chance survival of correspondence? The correspondence shows how wary the ecclesiastical authorities were about giving dissenters an opportunity to strengthen their position in society. It was an age of uneasy equilibrium between the established church and the dissenters. As regards Thomas Secker, he had already shown himself to be an indefatigable defender of orthodoxy. He was the son of a dissenter and had been destined for the dissenting ministry before he saw the error of his ways and, like many a convert, he became a champion of his adopted church's rights and privileges. The clamour to which constant reference was made in the correspondence doubtless refers to Friends' persistent opposition to the payment of tithes and their vigilance to secure favourable legislation. Had they not managed to secure exemption with Jews in Lord Hardwicke's Marriage Act, 1754? Secker was well aware of their attempts to promote legislation on tithes. As Bishop of Bristol, he had spoken in the House of Lords against the Quakers Tithe Bill in 1736, observing that Quakers 'plead a Scruple of Conscience against paying the Clergy what is due to them by the Law of the Land', but adding somewhat ingenuously: 'This you will agree is a very strange Scruple, and the stranger, because this very scrupulous People, who refuse paying to a Clergy, make no Scruple of paying to a War, though they reckon it just as Antichristian a Thing as a Clergy'. He also recalled how 'they meet every year in very large numbers & write circular Letters to all their Congregations, stirring up & exciting all their Friends in the strongest manner that words can express to disobey the Laws of the Land that require that Antichristian Payment of Tithes'[14]—a reference to Yearly Meeting and the epistle which certainly did exhort Friends to be mindful of their testimony against 'the Antichristian yoke of tithes'.

It was not only in Parliament that Secker was made aware of their activities. As a bishop, and later as Archbishop of Canterbury, he kept a close watch on their numbers. It was common for bishops to send out printed articles of enquiry to incumbents prior to visitation, containing questions about parish life, the numbers of parishioners, non-attenders and dissenters. But it was less common to enquire specifically about Quakers. Secker asked:

> Are there any Quakers in your Parish and how many? Is their Number lessened or increased of late Years, and by what means? Have they a Meeting House in your Parish duly licensed, and how often do they meet there? Do any of them, and how many in Proportion, pay you legal Dues without Compulsion? If not, do you lose such Dues? Or how do you recover them? And what Facts do you know, which may help to set their Behaviour towards the Clergy, or that of the Clergy towards them in a true light?[15]

How far can Joseph Sherwood be identified as a 'clamourous' Friend? From his early twenties, Sherwood's legal expertise singled him out for service to the Society. Perhaps one of his more significant appointments was his membership of the parliamentary committee of Meeting for Sufferings. He was first appointed 24 November 1758,[16] and from November

1760 until his death in 1773 he was a regular attender of the committee which included weighty and influential Friends such as John Fothergill, Henton Brown, Mark Beaufoy, Richard How and John Eliot. This committee was appointed annually at the beginning of each parliamentary session to 'take the necessary care respecting any bill or bills which may be brought into either House that will affect our Society'. In November 1759, possibly conscious of how dependent they had been on Richard Partridge for information, the parliamentary committee recommended that the best way of obtaining early intelligence of proposed legislation was to appoint a Friend to attend Parliament and to inform the committee as necessary. Richard How was appointed by Meeting for Sufferings to undertake this service.[17] On How's death in 1763, Joseph Sherwood seems to have kept a watching brief—as a colonial agent, he would have been familiar with parliamentary procedure and knowledgeable on proposed legislation. From December 1763, he paid over the customary annual fees of £11. 0s. 6d. to the clerks, doorkeepers and other officials of the Houses of Parliament.[18] In 1766, Meeting for Sufferings gratefully acknowledged 'the Care & Pains of our Friend Joseph Sherwood in attending the sessions of Parliament on this Meeting's Account'.[19] The following year, the Meeting showed its appreciation by allowing him ten guineas,[20] a sum which was thereafter given to him annually in recognition of this service.

In the years 1760-73, various Bills required the committee's attention, such as the Bills for rebuilding churches, the Marriage Bill 1765, the Militia Act 1764, the Stamp Act 1765. In a number of instances, the committee was able to report to Meeting for Sufferings its success in safeguarding Friends' interests. In 1767, it reported that two Friends had waited on the members of Parliament concerned with the Bill for rebuilding St Martin's, Worcester, with the request that Friends might be exempt from appointment as collectors or assessors of the church rate, and that the recovery of the rate payable by Friends might be restricted to the 'Justices warrant' (the Justices of the Peace would determine what was due and levy the amounts by distress). This was agreed to and a clause inserted in the Act.[21]

In view of the close ties between British and American Friends, the parliamentary committee took note of legislation affecting Friends in the colonies. In 1765, the Bill for the laying of stamp duties on the American colonies lacked provision for Friends to affirm instead of swearing an oath. The committee drafted a clause and asked Henton Brown, Mark Beaufoy and Peter Collinson to wait on George Grenville, the Chancellor of the Exchequer. These Friends were received with 'greatest marks of friendship', and Grenville readily agreed to the insertion of a clause relating to affirmation. Joseph Sherwood subsequently reported that the amended

Bill had been read in the House and provision made for Friends, 'tho' not by a single Clause'.[22]

Quite apart from responding to Bills read in the House, the committee promoted a Bill to mitigate the prosecution of Friends in the ecclesiastical courts or in the Courts of Exchequer for non-payment of tithes by extending the existing provision of recovery of tithes by justices warrant. The Bill was the outcome of a meeting between Friends and Sir Fletcher Norton, the newly appointed Speaker of the House of Commons, in 1772. It was customary to appoint a few Friends to wait on the new Speaker to request 'his favourable regard to our Society in any affairs that might come before the House respecting them', and on this occasion, the Speaker had intimated that 'they had so far the countenance of the Administration to be entitled to expect any marks of regard that could reasonably be expected or desired'. It was therefore with his encouragement that a Bill was drawn up and brought into the House; equally it was on his advice that the Bill was withdrawn once the opposition of the clergy appeared so strong that it was feared that Friends' sufferings were more likely to be increased than diminished by proceeding with the Bill.[23]

Sherwood was involved with this application to Parliament and may possibly have drafted the Bill, but he was not among the Friends appointed to consult with the Speaker or the Prime Minister: this was left to weightier Friends such as John Fothergill, Devereux Bowley and Jacob Hagen. That Meeting for Sufferings used his services as attorney is shown by records of payments of his 'attorney's bills'. Cases of Friends prosecuted in the Exchequer Court for non-payment of church dues were referred to him and, in some instances, he was employed to draw up cases for counsel's opinion. One such case concerned the unauthorised erection of a headstone by John Jefferys of Bath on his father's grave in the Quaker burial ground at Nailsworth, Glos. Since it was contrary to Friends' practice and considered to be 'introductive of great Inconveniences if the notion should prevail that every person may at pleasure enter forcibly into the Ground and bury the Dead or erect Tombs, etc., without the previous Licence of the Trustees', counsel's opinion was sought on whether to sue Jefferys. George Nares, barrister, of the Inner Temple (knighted 1771) opposed prosecution. He advised the removal of the stone, notice being given in writing to Jefferys that the stone had been improperly placed against the will of the Trustees and the known rules of the Society, and that 'he might have it back whenever he should think proper to send for it'.[24] By this means, Jefferys might be forced to bring an action himself and, if brought, it could not be maintained.

Apart from his many services on behalf of Meeting for Sufferings, Sherwood was also used by Six Weeks Meeting, the body of 'grave and antient Friends' principally responsible for the finance and property of London meetings. In view of his connection with Whitechapel where his father lived, and Wapping where he was articled in December 1748 to Thomas Cotton, attorney,[25] it is not surprising to find him being recommended to draw up the conveyances to new trustees of the Whitechapel burial ground and Wapping meeting house and burial ground in October 1756.[26] In 1758 he was employed to provide abstracts of title deeds belonging to the monthly meetings of Devonshire House, Horsleydown, Ratcliff and Westminster and to enter them in Six Weeks Meeting Book of Abstracts.[27] He was in fairly frequent demand as a conveyancer. Apart from professional work, he was appointed to the Meeting of Twelve, the predecessor of the Committee of Accounts, in November 1765,[28] and after having served what might be called his apprenticeship on this committee, he was appointed as one of the two representatives of Gracechurch Street Meeting on Six Weeks Meeting in February 1769.[29]

At a time when there were few Friends in the legal profession, Joseph Sherwood's training assured him a place in the Society's administration from an exceptionally young age. In 1757, when he could not have been more than twenty-three, he was sufficiently well known to be considered 'a proper person to do what business was left unfinished' on the death of the Recording Clerk, Jacob Post. For his work as a temporary assistant to the Recording Clerk, he received 12 guineas.[30] Joseph's commitment to the Society is not in doubt, but little light can so far be shed on his convincement: he was not a birthright Friend. Neither his father, John, described variously as a furrier and hair-cloth maker of Whitechapel,[31] nor his brother John who was articled to him in 1760,[32] were Quakers. By the time of his admission as attorney in King's Bench in 1754, he claimed membership of the Society, and when he was married he was a member of Peel Monthly Meeting, though he had moved sometime before within the compass of Gracechurch Street Monthly Meeting and had asked for his membership to be transferred some months before his wedding. This had been refused by Gracechurch Street: 'the minute, being deficient as to clearness of marriage, was rejected'.[33] Joseph Sherwood therefore requested to continue a member of Peel and did not finally transfer his membership until the late spring of 1758.[34]

By his marriage to Ann Wilson of Wandsworth, 2 December 1756,[35] Joseph Sherwood was brought into a close-knit group of Friends which was to include the Westons and Eliots. His wife was a birthright Friend, the daughter of William Wilson of Allendale, Northumberland. She was considerably older than him—he was about twenty-two and she was thirty-six. Their only child, Ann, was born in 1764,[36] and was orphaned by the age of nine. Joseph died of dropsy at the young age of thirty-nine, 1 June 1773,[37] and in his will, he gave thanks for 'all the mercies I have received from Almighty God' and recommended his soul 'to Almighty God earnestly beseeching him to forgive me all my sins through the sacrifice, mediation and atonement of the Blood of the Dear Son of His Love which I assuredly believe was shed on Mount Calvary for my sins . . .'.[38] He appointed as one of his executors the Quaker printer, Samuel Clark. Joseph's wife survived him by less than six months and, as her executors and guardians of their daughter, she chose Owen Weston of Wapping, her brother-in-law, and John Eliot, who had married Mary Weston in 1762.[39]

It is difficult to assess Sherwood's importance and, more particularly, his service to the Society. To judge from his letters relating to the colonial agency, he appears to have been a diligent and shrewd negotiator. He was realistic about his abilities to influence government policy once a course of action had been decided. He was willing to counsel caution and was a sound judge of human nature. He appreciated the constraints on government, especially when mistakes had been made. Writing in December 1768 about his endeavours to secure the repeal of various revenue acts which had met with strong opposition in the colonies, he observed: 'this government will not, at present, think it consistent with their dignity to repeal those acts, lest such a measure should be construed into a silent acknowledgment that they are not able to carry their acts into execution'.[40] His experience as agent for Rhode Island, 1759-73, and for New Jersey, c. 1761-66, made him an obvious candidate for appointment as a correspondent with Friends in America.

In the eighteenth century, there were many influential and wealthy Friends who gave their services to the Society and it was inevitable that in his youth he was overshadowed by them. Unlike many of them, he was not a recorded minister, neither does there appear to have been a testimony on his death. However his legal training, his understanding of the workings of government, combined with his experience gained from the colonial agency, made him a worthy servant of the Society. He amply justified the trust that Richard Partridge had in him in 1759 when he wrote: '. . . I am well perswaded his knowledge in Business, his prudent Conduct and Diligent application will give you ample Satisfaction'.[41]

NOTES

[1] Lambeth Palace Library, London (LPL): Secker Papers, 4, f.250.
[2] *Ibid.*, ff.250-61.
[3] LPL: Faculty Office *Fiats*, 1760/Sherwood (includes application, certificates, affirmation on appointment).

[4] John Russell Bartlett (ed.), *Records of the Colony of Rhode Island and Providence Plantations in New England* (Providence, 1861), 6, pp. 223, 226. For letter of agency see: Gertrude Selwyn Kimball (ed.), *The Correspondence of the Colonial Governors of Rhode Island, 1723-1775* (Boston & New York, 1903), 2, pp. 294-96.

[5] *Correspondence of the Colonial Governors*, 2, pp. 286-87.

[6] LPL: Faculty Office *Fiats*, 1732/Maude; Muniment Book, 1723-34, ff.168-69.

[7] Secker Papers, 4, ff.252-53.

[8] *Ibid.*, ff.254-55.

[9] *Ibid.*, f.257.

[10] See note 3 above.

[11] A.T.Gary, 'The Political and Economic Relations of English and American Quakers (1750-1785)' (D.Phil. thesis, University of Oxford, 1935), Appendix A, p. 456.

[12] Friends House Library (FHL): MS 'Records & Recollections of James Jenkins 1761 to 1821', p. 249.

[13] LPL: Faculty Office Muniment Book, 1754-1760, ff.241-42. The appointment had to be enrolled in Chancery.

[14] Secker Papers, 7, ff.326-33.

[15] LPL: Visitation returns, 1758, MS 1134/1-6.

[16] FHL: Minutes of Meeting for Sufferings (M/S): 30, p. 237. See also Minutes of the Parliamentary Committee, 1.

[17] Minutes of M/S, 30, p. 366.

[18] Minutes of M/S, 31, p. 256. See also Minutes of the Parliamentary Committee, 1, p. 33.

[19] Minutes of M/S, 31, p. 504.

[20] Minutes of M/S, 32, p. 99.

[21] *Ibid.* See also Minutes of the Parliamentary Committee, 1, pp. 47-48.

[22] Minutes of the Parliamentary Committee, 1, p. 38.

[23] Minutes of M/S, 33, pp. 90-97 (narrative of the proceedings in relation to the Tithe Bill).

[24] FHL: Book of Cases, 3, pp. 116-19. See also Minutes of M/S 31, p. 322; 32, p. 293.

[25] Public Record Office (PRO): Board of Inland Revenue Apprenticeship Books (Town), 18, p. 150.

[26] FHL: Minutes of London Six Weeks Meeting, 11, pp. 245, 250, 260.

[27] *Ibid.*, pp. 314, 322, 325, 328-29.

[28] Minutes of Six Weeks Meeting, 13, p. 102.

[29] *Ibid.*, p. 256.

[30] Minutes of M/S, 30, pp. 129, 169.

[31] FHL: Minutes of London Two Weeks Meeting, 8, p. 265 (reference to his consent to his son's marriage). Will of John Sherwood, 1764 (PRO: Prerogative Court of Canterbury (PCC) wills, Sampson 368).

[32] Board of Inland Revenue Apprenticeship Books (Town), 22, p. 88. See also application for admission as a notary, 1769: LPL Faculty Office *Fiats*, 1769/Sherwood.

[33] FHL: Minutes of Peel Monthly Meeting, 31/3/1756, 28/4/1756.

[34] *Ibid.*, 29/3/1758.

[35] FHL: Sussex & Surrey Quarterly Meeting Digest Registers, Marriages. See also London Two Weeks Meeting Minutes, 8, p. 265, and Book of Certificates, 1716-67, pp. 240-41.

[36] London & Middlesex Quarterly Meeting Digest Registers, Births.

[37] London & Middlesex Quarterly Meeting Digest Registers, Burials.

[38] PRO: PCC wills, Stevens 267.

[39] *Ibid.*, 489.

[40] *Records of the Colony of Rhode Island*, 6, pp. 571-72.

[41] *Correspondence of the Colonial Governors*, 2, pp. 286-87.

QUAKERS OBSERVED IN VERSE AND PROSE

by David Blamires

'That phanaticall, selfe-conceited sort of people called Quakers'—that was how Richard Gough saw them *c*.1701-02 when he wrote about the disreputable Richard Clarke in his now famous *History of Myddle*.[1] Only a few years earlier, on the occasion of her visit to Scarborough in 1697, Celia Fiennes, a more moderate observer, had this to say:

> I was at a Quakers Meeting in the town where 4 men and 2 women spoke, one after another had done, but it seem'd such a confusion and so incoherent that it very much moved my compassion and pitty to see their delusion and ignorance, and no less excited my thankfull-ness for the Grace of God that upheld others from such Errors; . . .[2]

Pepys, on learning of William Penn's return from Ireland in late 1667, wrote that he was 'a Quaker again, or some very melancholy thing; that he cares for no company, nor comes into any'.[3] Such comments come as no particular surprise to those even only moderately acquainted with the history of Quakerism in its first half-century, but modern readers will probably be unaware of the scurrilous picture of Quakers painted in popular verses and jokes well into the eighteenth century. These views of Friends do not pretend to any degree of historical accuracy or objectivity. Where resentment is caused by the actions of any group, comment on them is liable to be strongly partisan, distorted or full of innuendo. Valentine Cunningham has noted much the same kind of treatment of Dissent and Dissenters in the Victorian novel, with George Eliot providing a notable exception.[4] Writers do not always get their targets right; they frequently confuse the objects of their anger and derision with others who may share some, but not all of their general characteristics.

Dryden, in his satirical allegory *The Hind and the Panther* (1687), which treats of the religious debates and quarrels of his day, has much to say of Puritans, Roman Catholics and the Church of England, but dismisses Quakers summarily at the outset:

> Among the timorous kind the *Quaking Hare*
> Profess'd neutrality, but would not swear (i, 37-38).

In folklore the hare is not merely a timorous creature, it is also associated with witchcraft and with lechery. This last propensity was not uncommonly attributed to Quakers in the early days, to judge from popular songs and jokes. The opponents of Friends were quick to re-interpret Quaker reliance on the movement of the spirit as a cloak for engaging in illicit sexual intercourse. 'The Quaker's Song' in Thomas D'Urfey's *Pills to Purge Melancholy* (1719-20)[5] mocks Friends' ideals of purity and conscience by proposing hypocritical attitudes and motives of lustfulness. In five eight-line stanzas D'Urfey relates a Quaker seduction, justified by following the motions of the spirit, between 'a Holy Sister' and 'a Friend and a Brother'. (The terms 'Sister' and 'Brother' are used here metaphorically, not literally; the imputation is not one of incest.) The result of the seduction is, as one might expect, a pregnancy:

> But when the time was come,
>   That she was to be laid;
> It was not a very great Crime,
>   Committed by her they said:
> 'Cause they did know, and she did show,
>   'Twas done by a Friend and a Brother,
> But a very great Sin they said it had been,
>   If it had been done by another.

Two other ballads allege even more scandalous excesses on the part of a Quaker. 'News from Colchester' by Sir John Denham (1659) and 'The Four-legg'd Quaker', the latter published in *Wit and Mirth*, edited by H[enry] P[layford] (1682),[6] both lampoon one Ralph Green of Colchester, accusing him of sexual intercourse with a colt. 'News from Colchester' achieved considerable currency: it was reprinted in 1668, 1671 and 1684 and is referred to by John Gay in 'The Shepherd's Week' (Saturday, lines 109-12) (1714) and by Lady Mary Wortley Montagu in a letter to Lady Mar of November 1726.[7] The name of Ralph Green does not figure in the digests of births, marriages and deaths for Colchester Friends of this period,[8] but that does not allow us to dismiss the episode as unhistorical; it simply shrouds it in mystery. 'News from Colchester' invokes the names of both Fox and Nayler and ironically excuses the act of bestiality as 'meer impulse of Spirit,/Though he us'd the weapon carnal':

18

Now when in such a Saddle
A Saint will needs be riding,
    Though we dare not say
    'Tis a falling away,
May there not be some back-sliding?
No surely, quoth *James Naylor,*
'Twas but an insurrection
    Of the Carnal part,
    For a Quaker in heart
Can never lose perfection.

The doctrine that spiritual perfection was attainable on earth had provoked strong opposition to Fox in several places, and Nayler's trial for blasphemy and subsequent brutal punishment took place in the autumn of 1656. They must be understood as the public background facts to 'News from Colchester'.

'The Four-legg'd Quaker' focusses on the same incident as 'News from Colchester', making much play with puns on 'horse' and Horsley, 'colt' and Colchester. It vents its spleen chiefly on the Quakers, but refers also to a similar charge involving a Presbyterian woman and a dog. Throughout history religious dissent is generally associated with sexual licence by its detractors, and the refrain of 'The Four-legg'd Quaker' shouts loud the dangerous consequences for the position of the army, the means whereby the population at large is subject to control:

Help, Lords and Commons, once more help,
    O send us Knives and Daggers!
For if the Quakers be not Gelt
    Your Troopes will have the Staggers.

A second song in *Pills to Purge Melancholy,* 'The Penurious Quaker or, the High Priz'd Harlot',[9] takes Quaker lechery for granted, but adds to it a jibe at the Quaker's stinginess in paying for the whore's services. It also mocks the Quaker's reputation for truthfulness in the words put into his mouth:

I cannot like the Wicked say,
    I love thee and Adore thee,
And therefore thou wilt make me pay,
    So here is Six pence for thee.

Popular imputations of sexual licence are reflected, at least as far as the middle of the eighteenth century, in jokes circulated about Quakers. An Aldermary Church-Yard chapbook entitled *Cambridge Jests* (British Library, pressmark 1079.1.13.(10)) contains three jokes at the expense of Quakers, of which I quote one:

A Quaker having picked up a wench, carried her to a tavern, and treated her with burnt claret, of which they both drank very plentifully. The lady told the Quaker, That she must beg of him to look out at the window while she made water, for her modesty would not permit her to do it before a man. He gratified her. In the intrim *(sic)* she run down stairs with the fine silver boat in which they had their wine, and he was forced to pay for it.—Some time after, going with another Quaker, he said to his friend, It begins to rain hard, so we had best take a coach.—Ay, says the gentlewoman, who heard him, and knew the story, A coach will be cheaper to thee than a boat.

Indecorous twentieth-century counterparts to these early pasquinades against Quakers may be found in at least one limerick[10] and in the vulgar so-called 'Bugger's Alphabet',[11] but they lack the sharp focus and ostensible circumstantiality of the early material.

The earliest reference to a Quaker in fiction appears to be in *Bentivolio and Urania*, a religious romance by the Bristol writer Nathaniel Ingelo, first published in 1660 and reprinted in 1669, 1673 and 1682. The allusion is a local one—it is to James Nayler under the sobriquet of 'Jamnail'.[12] By the beginning of the eighteenth century, however, when Quakers had won their basic right to exist and had settled down to a quieter life, they begin to appear occasionally in a more favourable light in a variety of works. Addison and Steele continue to poke fun at them in their essays, but the contrast between Quaker plainness and the fussiness and pretence of the *beau monde* sometimes redounds to the Quakers' credit. In *The Spectator* of 1 August 1711 Steele provides an anecdote of a sober Quaker, Ephraim, who defends his guardian, a young lady, against the impudence of a captain, with whom the two, together with the young lady's mother, are travelling in a stage coach. The Quaker speaks out honestly and fearlessly, quells the captain's impertinences and yet retains his goodwill.[13] Steele had also written in *The Tatler* (no. 204, 29 July 1710) defending the Quaker practice of addressing all and sundry as 'Friend', contrasting this with the emptiness of honorific phrases widely used elsewhere.

The first major Quaker character in fiction seems to be William Walters in Defoe's *Life, Adventures and Pyracies of the Famous Captain Singleton* (1720).[14] William is a surgeon and taken by Singleton from a sloop bound from Pennsylvania to Barbadoes:

> He was a comick Fellow indeed, a Man of very good solid Sense, and an excellent Surgeon; but what was worth all, very goodhumour'd and pleasant in his Conversation, and a bold, stout, brave Fellow too, as any we had among us.[15]

Despite being engaged on a pirate ship William is no stage Quaker, simply there to provide a light-hearted note, but acts in ways that make him credible as a serious Quaker. He always avoids giving advice as to where the pirates should go, putting it off with 'some *Quaking* Quibble or other' (p. 188), but manages in indirect ways to moderate the pirates' tendency towards unnecessary violence. He pleads the cause of Negroes in a slaving ship, securing better treatment for them, but still participates in the slave trade. Singleton refers to him as 'Friend *William*, who was always for doing our Business without Fighting' (p. 235), and the two men become ever closer as they talk about death and repentance towards the end of the book. Their friendship is sealed by the captain giving bounty to William's sister and marrying her. Defoe obviously knew more about Quakers than simply the stereotypes. Although the book is more concerned with travel and adventure than with the study of human character, he paints in William the picture of a plausible individual rather than what might be regarded as a recognisable type.

A century later we can see rather more idealised traits in Scott's portrayal of Joshua Geddes in *Redgauntlet* (1824). He is clearly a foil to the rough, venturesome and ruthless Herries of Birrenswork, otherwise known as Redgauntlet, and is described in some detail when he enters the story. His clothing shows him to be a Friend. This 'merciful man' who is merciful to his horse has accoutrements that are 'in the usual unostentatious, but clean and serviceable order, which characterizes these sectaries'. He has

> a comely and placid countenance, the gravity of which appeared to contain some seasoning of humour, and had nothing in common with the pinched puritanical air affected by devotees in general. The brow was open and free from wrinkles, whether of age or hypocrisy. The eye was clear, calm, and considerate, . . . (letter VI).

Joshua and his sister Rachel live in five or six acres of land that their father, with 'a considerable taste for horticulture', has formed into a variety of gardens that are now a 'little Eden of beauty, comfort, and peace'. Darsie Latimer writes:

> If the house at Mount Sharon be merely a plain and convenient dwelling, of moderate size, and small pretensions, the gardens and offices, though not extensive, might rival an earl's in point of care and expense (letter VII).

Joshua deprecates Darsie's angling for pure pleasure, while he himself catches salmon for food. Scott adds various other touches to his Quaker portrait, but in depicting Joshua's exasperation at the devilment of the boy Benjie he is clever enough to temper idealism with a realistic dash of human frailty. Even the placid Quaker can lose his cool.

Scott's description of Rachel Geddes draws attention to 'the most perfect neatness and cleanliness of her dress; and her simple close cap was particularly suited to eyes which had the softness and simplicity of the dove's'. She also possesses 'a pleasing sobriety of smile, that seemed to wish good here and hereafter to every one she spoke to' (letter VII). That takes us back to *The Spectator* again, in which Tickell dilates, in the number for 10 December 1714, on a pretty young Quaker woman in a coach:

> ... the pretty Quaker appeared in all the Elegance of Cleanliness. Not a Speck was to be found upon her. A clear, clean, oval Face, just edged about with little thin Plaits of the purest Cambrick, received great Advantages from the Shade of her black Hood; as did the Whiteness of her Arms from that sober coloured Stuff in which she had Clothed her self. The Plainness of her Dress was very well suited to the Simplicity of her Phrases; all which, put together, though they could not give me a great Opinion of her Religion, they did of her Innocence.

The modest decorousness of Quaker women is a characteristic often adverted to by novelists and commentators over a century and half or more, but nowhere does it strike the reader in a more extraordinary context than that in which George Borrow, in *Lavengro* (1851), writes about suicide:

> I remember a female Quaker who committed suicide by cutting her throat, but she did it decorously and decently: kneeling down over a pail, so that not one drop fell upon the floor; thus exhibiting in her last act that nice sense of sweetness for which Quakers are distinguished. I have always had a respect for that woman's memory (chapter XXIII).

Quakers in general tend to be depicted respectfully in nineteenth-century fiction, quite in contrast to the treatment widely handed out to Methodists and other Dissenters.[16] That does not mean that they are always portrayed as faultless. In *John Halifax, Gentleman* (1857) Mrs Craik shows the stern and rough aspects of Phineas's father, Abel Fletcher, who believes that 'plenty was not good for the working-classes; they required to be kept low' (chapter II) and separates the two boys, Phineas and John Halifax, in their friendship because of an unsanctioned visit to the theatre. The period referred to is the 1790s, as is also the case in Mrs Gaskell's *Sylvia's Lovers* (1863), where we are introduced to the two Quaker brothers who keep a shop devoted to grocery, drapery and mercery in the coastal town of Monkshaven. They keep their shop open at Christmas, ignoring that Christian festival, but entertain their customers to cake and wine on New Year's Day. They also provide a primitive banking service. 'Yet, though scrupulous in most things, it did not go against the consciences of these good brothers to purchase smuggled articles' (chapter III).

Clearly, it would be possible to add very considerably to these few examples of attitudes towards Quakers in nineteenth-century writings. Most people are familiar with Charles Lamb's essays on 'A Quakers' Meeting' and 'Imperfect Sympathies', where he sets out his admiration for Quaker ways and worship, while at the same time noting his reservations about the restrictions imposed by their simple tastes (*Essays of Elia* (1823)). The image of Quaker sobriety and rectitude was spread during the nineteenth-century by such small things as the children's alphabet books that insisted: 'Q was a Quaker, who would not bow down',[17] and:

> Q Was a Quaker both stiff and upright,
> In yea and in nay, they chiefly delight.[18]

Most alphabet books represent Q by a queen, usually of the ceremonial kind, but William Nicholson's superb *Alphabet* of the very end of the century (1898), designed perhaps more for art-lovers than for children, provides a fine example of the traditional Quaker man, sitting on a chair, in a costume that had long since disappeared as a means of distinguishing Quakers from other people.

How different then are twentieth-century Quakers in fiction? There are many more of them than I can mention here, but let me simply note in passing the pervasive American Quaker setting of Christopher Isherwood's *The World in the Evening* (1952) and the conscientious objector Andrew, working as a ward orderly in a military hospital, in Mary Renault's sensitive novel about the different ways in which three men experience homosexual love and try to deal with it—*The Charioteer* (1953). I want to conclude by looking at one very recent novel.

The Philosopher's Pupil (1983) is unusual among Iris Murdoch's novels in that several of the principal figures are Quakers. It is entirely usual in most other respects: its characters are largely middle-class, well-educated and unworried by economic and political problems; their personal relationships and changing passions constitute the chief purpose of their lives; there are a variety of wayward religious and philosophical figures who provide an opportunity for moral and spiritual reflexions.

The novel is set in Ennistone, a town whose chief features seem to be a compound of Bath (the hot springs) and Cheltenham (Burkestown reminds one of Pittville). The family that provides the chief characters, the McCaffreys, were 'originally commercially minded Quakers' (Penguin edition, p. 35), but it is only Brian and Gabriel who are given any recognisable Quaker characteristics:

> [Brian] did not believe in God, but the Ennistone Friends were not anxious about this matter. The Mystery of God was one with the Inner Light of the Soul, and the illumined Way was the Good Life,

where truthful vision spontaneously prompted virtuous desire. Herein lay the perfect simplicity of duty. Brian pictured himself as austere and pure in heart. He wanted to live the Good Life with his wife and his son, but he found this difficult (pp. 59-60).

Brian is selfish, bossy with his wife, irascible, awkward with his son, certainly no paragon of Quaker ideals. His wife Gabriel is an inveterate worrier, constantly attempting to reconcile people and alleviate distress. On the occasion of the disastrous seaside picnic her attempts to save a fish in a tiny rockpool by giving two pounds to a couple of uncouth teenagers to put it back in the sea provide a note of comedy mingled with pain. Tom McCaffrey, Brian's much younger half-brother, the 'young hero' of the novel, goes to meeting sometimes and, when interrogated by the philosopher Rozanov, declares: "'It means something to me'" (p. 270). What precisely it means he does not go into, nor does the novel give much further clue.

The Quakers of Ennistone are well-to-do people, by and large, though any conspicuous wealth appears to be in the past, not the present. The pivotal Quaker character in the novel is William Eastcote:

> (popularly known as 'Bill the Lizard'), a very devout person and pillar of the Meeting, and a cousin of the well-known philanthropist Milton Eastcote. The Eastcotes were a wealthy family (also originally 'in trade') and William retired early from a career at the bar to devote himself, like his cousin, to good works (p. 59).

He is the unofficial 'philosopher' in the novel, the counterpart to John Robert Rozanov, the successful academic philosopher whom everyone wants to have a connexion with and who is so comically hopeless when it comes to human relationships (Rozanov was originally a Methodist). The two men are actually good friends, and their two deaths conclude the novel. Rozanov and the consequences of his return to his native Ennistone furnish the central action of the book, but William Eastcote, though in a way tangential, makes a number of critical appearances. He is an archetypal 'wise man' whose quality of life makes a difference to everybody with whom he comes into touch.

There are three Quaker 'set pieces' in the novel—an account of the meeting for worship at which William Eastcote, conscious of his impending death, gives his last ministry; a description of his funeral; and a brief comment on Tom and Hattie's Quaker wedding. The first of these is the most important. The omniscient narrator explores the rambling thoughts of several of the worshippers, first setting the scene in the handsome eighteenth-century meeting house. There are about twenty worshippers, all identified by name, but only William Eastcote rises to give vocal ministry, his heart beating hard because he is a diffident speaker. His ministry centres on a call to 'love the close things, the close clear good things, and hope that in their light other goods may be added' (p. 204). He praises innocence, idealism, chastity as 'a sense of the delicate mystery of human relations', and counsels his hearers to shun cynicism, malice and despair. Everyone afterwards resolves to mend the faults and damages in their immediate lives.

William's funeral, which takes place in the all-purpose chapel next to the municipal graveyard, is oddly silent:

> The gathering was not large. All the Ennistone Friends were there, and a few others including Milton Eastcote. No one was moved to speak. Any eulogy of the deceased was felt to be unnecessary and out of place. Many people wept quietly in the silence (p. 472).

Afterwards the coffin is carried to the grave, where nearly two thousand people

> stood in complete and impressive silence through the duration (almost half an hour) of the meeting, and only pushed forward a little during the interment. Afterwards, and quite spontaneously (it is not known who started it) this large crowd sang *Jerusalem*, a favourite of William's . . . (p. 472).

On hearing of William's death, several of the main characters feel that they ought to have discussed their problems with him before and that he would have given the catalytic advice they needed. This is in complete contrast to Rozanov, the reclusive philosopher, whose actions are frequently misinterpreted and bring turmoil to all with whom he comes into contact.

Iris Murdoch presents Quakers and Quakerism in an attractive light in *The Philosopher's Pupil*. She has got the descriptive details right, and the range of beliefs and attitudes that she attributes to Brian and Gabriel McCaffrey, William Eastcote and the other members of Ennistone Meeting are entirely plausible. Brian's tacit atheism is counterbalanced by William's explicitly Christian words. And Nesta Wiggins's worry that 'the money voted for the repainting of the Meeting House ought instead to be donated to the recently opened appeal for the new community centre on the wasteland beyond the canal' (p. 203) must—apart from the use of the word 'voted'—evoke memories of many a Quaker discussion about premises and money. The picture is sympathetic, but not sentimental; it rings true to life, and William Eastcote's ministry will seem to many readers an admirable incapsulation of basic Quaker values. Iris Murdoch's view of Friends is a far cry from Richard Gough's sharp condemnation and Sir John Denham's cheerful scorn.

The changing images of Quakers in verse and prose, in fiction and passing comment by non-Friends in diaries, essays, autobiographies and the like, could be much more extensively documented than I have had space for in this short sketch. I have, for example, deliberately omitted the American scene and not mentioned either Voltaire or Dr Johnson, whose views of Friends are excerpted in Bernard Canter's *Quaker Bedside Book* (1952). I hope, nonetheless, that what I have selected gives a fair cross-section of the ways in which Quakers have come across to their fellow-citizens over more than three hundred years. There is room somewhere for a whole book on the subject, and perhaps an anthology.[19]

NOTES

[1] *The History of Myddle*, by Richard Gough, edited by David Hey (Harmondsworth: Penguin Books, 1981), p. 172.

[2] *The Journeys of Celia Fiennes*, edited by Christopher Morris (London: Cresset Press, 1947), pp. 92-93.

[3] *The Illustrated Pepys. Extracts from the Diary*, edited by Robert Latham (London: Bell & Hyman, 1978), p. 168.

[4] Valentine Cunningham, *Everywhere Spoken Against. Dissent in the Victorian Novel* (Oxford: Clarendon Press, 1975).

[5] Reprinted in *The Common Muse: an Anthology of Popular British Ballad Poetry, 15th-20th Century*, edited by Vivian de Sola Pinto and Allan Edwin Rodway (Harmondsworth: Penguin Books, 1965), pp. 467-68.

[6] 'News from Colchester' is reprinted in *Poetical Works of Sir John Denham*, edited by Theodore Howard Banks, Jr. (New Haven, 1928), pp. 91-94; 'The Four-legg'd Quaker' in *The Common Muse* (see note 5 above), pp. 472-77.

[7] See *The Complete Letters of Lady Mary Wortley Montagu*, edited by Robert Halsband (Oxford: Clarendon Press, 1965-67), vol. II, pp. 71-72.

[8] See Stanley Henry Glass Fitch, *Colchester Quakers* (Colchester, 1962), p. 147.

[9] Reprinted in *The Common Muse* (see note 5 above), p. 480.

[10] See *The Limerick*, edited by G.Legman (Frogmore: Panther Books, 1976), vol. II, p. 33.

[11] See *The Bawdy Beautiful: the Sphere Book of Improper Verse*, edited by Alan Bold (London: Sphere Books, 1979), pp. 41-43.

[12] '"William the Quaker" or the Friend in Fiction', *Journal of the Friends Historical Society*, 13 (1916), p. 59, note 1.

[13] See 'The Friend in Fiction', *Journal of the Friends Historical Society*, 13 (1916), pp. 171-74. The new edition of *The Spectator* by Donald F.Bond (Oxford: Clarendon Press, 1965) attributes this piece to Steele, not Addison.

[14] See '"William the Quaker"' (see note 12 above), pp. 59-61.

[15] Quotations from the reprint published Oxford: Blackwell; Stratford-upon-Avon: Shakespeare Head Press, 1927.

[16] See Cunningham, *op. cit.*, *passim*.

[17] See *Tom Thumb's Alphabet* (London: William Darton and Son, *c*.1830) and *The Child's Coloured Gift Book* (London: Routledge, 1867).

[18] See *The Silver Penny* (York: J.Kendrew, mid-nineteenth century), reprinted in *Chapbook ABCs*, edited by Peter Stockham (New York: Dover Publications, 1974).

[19] I am grateful to David J.Hall for bringing to my attention over several years a large variety of references to Quakers in literary sources.

CUSHIONS ON EVERY OTHER BENCH: A BASIS FOR 'RAPPROCHEMENT' AMONG AMERICAN FRIENDS

by Thomas R. Bodine

When I was a boy growing up in the Orthodox Coulter Street Meeting in Germantown, Philadelphia, I remember chuckling over what may have been an apocryphal argument among Friends in that meeting some time in the 1870s. The story went that they had argued heatedly for years over whether they should continue to worship on hard wooden benches, as they had done since the meeting was founded in 1681, or should they put cushions on their benches which some felt would be more conducive to effective worship. After years of disagreement and dispute, they finally arrived at a decision that all could unite with: they put cushions on every other bench. It was a purely trivial matter, but the decision finally reached left individuals, or families, free to decide for themselves which basis of seating was best, and it didn't inflict on others a basis of seating not best for them.

A similar decision was reached by New England Friends in 1945 when the two New England Yearly Meetings reunited into a single Yearly meeting——after precisely a hundred years of separation. The pastoral and programmed 'Yearly Meeting of Friends for New England', and the non-pastoral, unprogrammed 'New England Yearly Meeting of Friends' came together, partly at the insistence of the rapidly growing 'new and united' unaffiliated local meetings that had sprung up in the Connecticut Valley and at Cambridge and Providence. These generally liberal, service-oriented, often humanist groups of Friends did not want to join either or both of the two separated Yearly Meetings. In Henry Cadbury's phrase, 'They didn't want to become the adopted children of divorced parents'.

There had been joint committees to explore the possibilities of reunion in New England as far back as 1937. The first such committee tried unsuccessfully for five years to come up with a formula that would permit Friends of differing beliefs and practices to work and worship together. The main stumbling block was what form of worship should take place on the Sunday morning of Yearly Meeting and in the daily worship groups during the week. Should it be programmed worship or unprogrammed worship? The second joint committee, appointed in 1942, had a bright idea. Why not have a variety of types of worship in the daily morning groups, with individual Friends free to choose which to attend, and on the Sunday, when the whole Yearly Meeting would want to worship together, the form of worship could alternate from year to year, one year with a full programme of hymns, bible-reading, and a prepared sermon, and the next year unprogrammed on the basis of silence? This was a landmark decision and gives us a clue as to a possible basis for *rapprochement* among all American Friends today including the far-out Evangelicals.

There was another respect in which the reunion of the two Yearly Meetings in New England in 1945 contributed to *rapprochement*. The former Gurneyite body in New England was already a member of the Five Years Meeting, and it was decided that that membership should be continued when the Yearly Meetings reunited. That decision swung a number of unprogrammed Friends from the 'new and united' meetings and from the former Wilburite body into the operation of the pastoral, 'main-line-Church' Five Years Meeting in Richmond, Indiana (which in 1960 changed its name to Friends United Meeting). And under the pressure of the 'new and united' meetings, the reunited Yearly Meeting soon joined the liberal Friends General Conference in Philadelphia, and that meant that a number of bible-based, Christ-centred programmed Friends from the former Gurneyite body in New England found themselves attending gatherings of Hicksite Friends at Cape May, New Jersey and later at Ithaca, New York and at Slippery Rock, Pennsylvania. The *rapprochement* of the Orthodox and Hicksite, Gurneyite and Wilburite Friends was under way.

The separated Hicksite-Orthodox Yearly Meetings in New York, Baltimore and Canada soon followed New England's example, and both the Five Years Meeting (Friends United Meeting) and the Friends General

Conference felt themselves enriched by the influx of Friends from the other branches of Quakerism.

The two Yearly Meetings in Philadelphia took the step in 1955. They had been at it longer than any of the other reunited yearly meetings, with endless joint committees and work projects and conferences and Young Friends' gatherings and Discipline-drafting groups over the years since the beginning of the twentieth century, which led William Bacon Evans to comment, when objection was raised in 1955 to the decision to go ahead and reunite:

> Friends should move carefully, but I don't think waiting 100 years is moving too fast.

By the time of the great Conference of Friends in the Americas held in 1957, the *rapprochement* among Hicksite, Orthodox and 'main-line' Friends was practically complete. It was at a conference held at Wilmington, Ohio in the very same year that the last of the Evangelical Separations took place, when a group of Friends in Nebraska Yearly Meeting withdrew from the Five Years Meeting and formed the extremely evangelical Rocky Mountain Yearly Meeting. To illustrate the possible basis for unity among Friends of differing points of view, let me quote from the report prepared by the worship-fellowship groups at that 1957 Conference of Friends in the Americas, a report which I helped to draw up:

> We are grateful for the opportunity to know and better understand the differences which exist among us. These differences are very real and very difficult, but in the struggle to share the intimate personal experiences that have built our faith, in reviewing together the problems of individuals as they seek to apply their faith, in the struggle to get to know each other at deep levels, we have found unity.

> We have called it an 'experiential' unity, a unity that we have experienced for ourselves through the phenomenon of the Holy Spirit. As we worshipped together the differences represented by our name tags and labels melted away . . .

> We believe that experiential unity need not involve uniformity, but may be nurtured by our variety. We believe that widely differing approaches actually stimulate the growth of a group that is seeking under the guidance of the Holy Spirit.

I find these words as valid today as when they were written over twenty-five years ago.

But the Evangelicals were not officially represented at that 1957 Conference. If they had been, we would not have been able to release such a statement in the name of the Conference, a statement that made no mention of Jesus Christ and his Saving Grace!

At about this time, however, the annual gathering of Quaker pastors and meeting secretaries established the Quaker Theological Discussion Group, which to this day has published a journal called *Quaker Religious Thought*, presenting many points of view across the whole theological spectrum of Friends.

Also about this time the Earlham School of Religion was established in Richmond, Indiana, to train Friends for leadership in the Society not just as pastors but also as meeting secretaries and as staff persons or as teachers in the myriad Quaker service and educational institutions around the world, or simply to train Friends for leadership in their local meetings, much as Woodbrooke tries to do.

In 1967 the fourth Friends World Conference was held at Guildford, North Carolina. This was also a landmark occasion when Friends of all kinds and descriptions met one another in small groups and learned that whereas words divide, worship unites. This conference the Evangelicals did attend.

Hugh Doncaster delivered the keynote address. It is a pity to quote only a sentence or two from one of Hugh's talks, particularly one delivered in an atmosphere of worship, but what electrified the one thousand Friends assembled that evening, 75% of whom came from pastoral meetings, was to hear him say:

> I believe the pastoral system to be a backward-pointing by-pass off the main road of essential Quakerism.

But in the next breath, he said:

> [But that] is trivial, I believe, compared to a much more insidious mood, which is prevalent in London Yearly Meeting—a mood of vague permissiveness which affects both matters of belief and social witness and moral testimony . . . And this I believe is a far more serious ill . . . than the [pastoral system].

On the subject of the Quaker faith, he said:

> There is in the heart of every single human person something of the spirit of the Christ-like God himself at work. And if you prefer to say 'For God so loved the world that He sent His only begotten Son that whosoever believes on Him should not perish but have eternal life', is this not trying to say in other words what I [have just] said in the idiom . . . of more liberal Friends?

30

In 1972, there were two evangelical Friends on the Nominating Committee that invited me to become the Presiding Clerk of Friends United Meeting, one of whom was the pastor of Richard Nixon's Quaker church in East Whittier, California. They asked me 'Tom, are you a Christian? Have you been saved?' I answered, 'Yes'. In my terminology I felt that I was at least trying to lead a Christ-like life and that I had experienced in worship the sensation of feeling the evil in me weakening and the good lifted up, which I take it is the same religious experience as the sensation of feeling washed clean of my sins in the Blood of the Lamb. I would simply use different words to describe the same religious experience.

I had no sooner taken over as Clerk of Friends United Meeting in 1972 than we were faced with a decision about Sunday-school materials. The supplies were running out and they were out-of-date anyway. We must decide at once: what printed materials should be made available to Sunday-school teachers throughout the FUM: a bible-based, Christ-centred curriculum, which would not be acceptable to liberal Friends in its over-emphasis on biblical authority—or a testimony-based, Jesus-as-Teacher-and-Friend type of curriculum, which would not of course be acceptable to Evangelical Friends? The impasse seemed insurmountable. So we abandoned the attempt and settled into two days of worship, some of it programmed, some unprogrammed. And out of it we came up with the idea of a two-track curriculum, one bible-based, Christ-centred, the other testimony-oriented, Jesus-as-Teacher-and-Friend, with each local meeting throughout the FUM free to choose one or the other, or as in the case of my home meeting in Hartford, Connecticut, to choose something from each. This willingness to recognise the validity of the other Friends' Quakerism or Christianity, instead of denouncing it as un-Quakerly or non-Christian, was I think a giant step forward for the Society of Friends in the Americas. It was rather like the Coulter Street Friends deciding to put cushions on every other bench, or the reunited New England Yearly Meeting deciding to have a variety of forms of worship in their daily morning worship groups. Each Friend or local meeting was free to choose for themselves under the guidance of the Holy Spirit.

In my final year as Clerk of FUM in 1975, the question of a statement of the Quaker faith came to a head. For twenty-five years from 1950 to 1975 evangelical Friends had tried to get the FUM to agree on a statement of some sort. The Evangelicals felt that Friends should certainly, somehow, be able to say what they believed. In the 1950s the Evangelicals brought forward the 'Richmond Declaration of Faith' drafted with the help of English Friends in 1887 which a minute written by Rufus Jones in 1922 had described as 'documents which gather up and express the central truths for which we stand, now as in the past'. Could not Friends agree on it as the basis of their faith? But liberal and even 'main-line' Friends found it much too credal in character.

In the 1960s a study group representing all the varieties of Friends was appointed and after several years of earnest and arduous work came up with an equally long document entitled, 'An Affirmation of Faith and Life for Friends United Meeting'. This was much less rigid than the 'Richmond Declaration of Faith' and consisted of language reflecting both the evangelical and liberal points of view. But the fear of credal statements and the apparent Christian exclusiveness of the document and its inordinate length prevented its adoption.

In 1972 the Evangelicals tried again, this time with a very short and simple statement:

> It is our firm conviction that the foundation of and the basis for membership in Friends United Meeting is rooted in Jesus Christ, as biblically revealed, historically understood, and presently experienced; that His Saviourhood and Lordship should be central to our faith and life; and that we should seek to live out the implications of this reality under the guidance and power of the Holy Spirit.

The Evangelicals could not understand why this simple statement of faith was not acceptable to the Liberals and in 1975 they threatened to withdraw if we were unable to unite on some statement that could be cited as the official position of Friends United Meeting. What to do? Were we headed for another Separation?

A year or two before, one of the evangelical yearly meetings had come up with the idea that the 'Richmond Declaration of Faith' adopted by the Five Years Meeting as a basis of unity in 1902 had never been rescinded and was therefore still the official statement of Friends United Meeting, although not the position of a number of its constituent yearly meetings. Some historical research through seventy years of minutes (how many minutes in a Quaker hour?) established that this was indeed so. The FUM already *had* an official statement and we need not try to write a new one. The minute I drafted as Clerk of FUM in 1975 which was adopted in a spirit of love and unity reads as follows:

> We have felt in our meetings together to consider this subject the same overshadowing presence of the Holy Spirit that Friends felt in 1922 . . .

> We accept the findings of this research into the origins and present status of the 'Richmond Declaration of Faith' and related documents and recognise that the 'Authorised Declaration of Faith' reaffirmed in 1922 remains the official statement of Friends United Meeting.

We note the conditions under which it was adopted. It is our under-standing that these conditions left constituent Yearly Meetings free to be guided by their own inspiration and did not impose a particular phraseology on staff or officers of Friends United Meeting.

In the words of a Young Friend addressing the sessions: 'It's been a great experience to examine our faith. Let's do it some more. And now let's see if we can live by it.'

Copies of the 'Richmond Declaration of Faith' were reprinted in a modern binding and a special edition of London Yearly Meeting's book of *Christian Faith and Practice* was run off and both items were circulated widely throughout the 1,500 local meetings that make up Friends United Meeting.

In the years following the Friends World Conference of 1967, several steps toward *rapprochement* were taken among American Friends. In 1970 the Evangelicals called on every yearly meeting to send five representa-tives each to St Louis 'for a national conference to seek, under the guidance of the Holy Spirit, a workable, challenging and co-operative means whereby the Friends Church can be an active, enthusiastic, Christ-centred and Spirit-directed Force in this day of revolution.' Most American yearly meetings sent representatives to St Louis and they had a great time together even though they could agree only on establishing a 'Faith and Life Panel' to go on looking at the issues raised and to come together again in a second Faith and Life Conference at Indianapolis in 1974. Again in 1974 they were unable to reach any agreement except that they should look for opportunities to meet and worship together and should continue the work of the 'Faith and Life Panel' which published in 1978 a study book entitled *Quaker Worship in North America*, edited by Francis B. Hall.

Since Friends did not seem to be getting very far in arriving at a common statement of the Quaker faith, the Evangelicals proposed, with the sup-port of the Section of the Americas of the Friends World Committee, that they should have a try at working together on a common project in which all Friends could unite, however divided they might be in beliefs and practices. All yearly meetings in the United States and Canada subscribe to the Peace Testimony. The decidely evangelical California Yearly Meet-ing, for example, includes an emphasis on peace in the leaflet it uses to describe the faith and practice of Friends to visitors and applicants for membership:

As Friends we believe the Bible is our outward rule of Faith; Jesus Christ is the Word become flesh for us; the Holy Spirit is our strengthener; God is our Father.

We emphasise the immediacy of Christ and His availability, without rite or ritual to all who will believe. Our thrust is evangelistic and missionary and we also believe there is a better way to settle disputes than by fighting. Therefore we pray and we work for peace. And we say to all men everywhere: LET'S BE FRIENDS.

And so there went out a 'New Call to Peacemaking', in which Friends from across the whole spectrum, together with representatives of the other historic peace churches, the Brethren and the Mennonites, met together first in regional conferences in 1977, then in October 1978 at a great representative gathering assembled at Green Lake, Wisconsin, and in other forums to the present day.

Following the Friends World Conference of 1967, the Friends World Committee for Consultation at the world level took up the cause of *rapprochement* by sponsoring a succession of Mission and Service Conferences in 1973, 1976 and 1979 to discuss the major evangelical Quaker thrust of missionary work throughout the world and the major liberal Quaker thrust of service work throughout the world. These were often in conflict with one another so that the following specific recommendation from the 1973 gathering was a significant step forward:

> WE RECOMMEND that any Quaker agency intending to work in a country where another Quaker agency is already involved, should consult that body.

The spirit of these Mission and Service Conferences is well expressed in a report from the second one, in 1976:

> In our worship and sharing together we have come to a new level of appreciation for the authenticity and integrity of one another.

> After a time of frank, open and loving sharing of the basic issues that tend to divide Friends throughout the world, an enlightenment of our understanding of these issues has seemed to clear away inhibitions and stereotypes heretofore prevalent and damaging to co-operative mission and service efforts.

It has to be said that from its beginning in 1937, the Friends World Committee at the world level has been dominated by liberal and 'mainline' Friends, with only token participation by the Evangelicals. This is partly due to the unfriendly attitude over the years of many British, Continental and Australasian Friends to the faith and practice of the Evangelicals with their emphasis on evangelism and missionary work, their respect for biblical authority and the centrality of Christ, and their employment of pastors and a programmed form of worship. It is so easy to denounce 'those other Friends' as not proper Quakers, just as it is easy for the Evangelicals to denounce Friends at the other end of the spectrum as non-Christian and 'unsound'.

At the Thirteenth Meeting of the Friends World Committee held in Canada in 1976, a gesture was made towards the Evangelicals and towards the half of the world population of Friends deeply concerned for mission programmes, by changing the constitution of the World Committee to add to its aims and purposes the words:

> To keep under review the Quaker contribution . . . to the world Christian mission.

Nothing much has come of this constitutional recognition of the world-wide Quaker concern for Christian mission, and it is interesting to note that the London *Friend*, in reporting on the Thirteenth Triennial, omitted any reference to this addition of 'Christian mission' to the World Committee's aims and purposes.

A description of the *rapprochement* taking place among American Friends would be remiss to omit any reference to the Conference of all Friends in the Americas held in Wichita, Kansas, in June 1977, the first time in 150 years that an open meeting of all the different varieties of American Quakers was held at one time in one place. This 1977 Conference had a lower attendance than expected. Only 900 Friends came to it when over 1,500 had been expected, and it consequently cost the sponsoring Quaker agencies sizeable sums of money. Friends from the extremist wings (liberal and evangelical) showed up in some numbers, but the 'main-line', middle-of-the-road Friends mostly stayed at home or sent their pastors to represent them. Some better understanding among Friends of different persuasions was achieved and the Spanish-speaking Quakers from South and Central America discovered each other for the first time, and have set up an organisation under the sponsorship of the Section of the Americas of the Friends World Committee to continue in communication.

What lessons can we draw from these *rapprochement* experiences taking place among American Friends in the twentieth century? Certainly one is that Friends of differing views about Quaker faith and practice can unite in worship and can unite in working together on projects of common concern. Another is that we must somehow learn to live with the tensions created by differing views of faith and practice. We need to recognise that the differing views reflected in the American divisions are fundamentally irreconcilable, that one cannot expect agreement between Hicksites and the Orthodox, or between the humanist and the Christ-centred, or between the programmed and the unprogrammed. These positions, which I feel are all valid forms of Quakerism, are truly irreconcilable. It is simply not possible to agree on a statement of faith or on a Sunday-school curriculum or on the form of worship at a re-united yearly meeting, or even on whether to worship on cushions or on hard wooden benches. The only way to be Friends is to set forth the differing views and then leave individuals and meetings free to choose for themselves under the guidance of the Holy Spirit.

Quakers by their very nature are individualist and many have come to Friends to escape the rigidities of their former church connection. Many, at all points along the spectrum, are 'upright' in their views: rigid, harsh, strong-minded. Matters of faith and practice have to be 'either-or'; they cannot be 'both-and'. What is needed, of course, is patience, openness, readiness to hear the other out—in a word: love. As Daisy Newman puts it in her great history of American Quakerism, *A Procession of Friends:*

> The very strength of character which earlier [had] made Friends heroic [and] willing to suffer for their convictions [may] now [make] them uncompromising and wanting in charity.

Caring is the greatest thing; caring matters most.

Either we can learn to respect the other's sincerity and respect the validity of the other's point of view, or we can reconcile ourselves to disunity and division. We can draw a circle that rules out 'those other Friends' or we can draw a circle that rules them in. Our differences of faith and practice are like vases into which we are putting flowers, different flowers, different vases, but the water essential to the life of all the flowers is the spirit of God.

What I long for in Quakerism and what I have worked for all my life is that we should recognise the validity of the other's form of faith and practice and discover the true unity that underlies the differences of the language we use to describe our religious experience. Above all, in the words of California Yearly Meeting, 'LET'S BE FRIENDS'.

THE RAMBLINGS OF A RECORDING CLERK

by Geoffrey Bowes

A Friend who recently saw me giving some attention to one of the plants on a landing in Friends House remarked: 'Oh for a camera to record the duties of the Recording Clerk!' He was wrong; it was not a duty but an act of love. The duties of the Recording Clerk are manifold but the care of the plants in Friends House or in the garden is not among them. Yet, that Friend's chance remark has led me to reflect upon the links which can be established between my responsibilities, I will not persist with the word duties, as Recording Clerk, and my other more private life and love as a gardener.

They are not obvious. It is true that when I first came to Friends House I dreamed of donning overalls at lunchtime and digging and delving in the garden, emulating earlier Friends such as Lilian Impey and John Robson who took time off from the compelling round of 'committee week' to supplement the labours of the porters in tending the Friends House garden. However, it has remained a dream. The nearest I have come to having my spice and my ha'penny was when, as Assistant Recording Clerk, for a time I carried responsibility for the newly established Premises & Services Department. The comparatively recent plantings in the courtyard may prove to be a lasting memorial to this period, yet even there it was only the idea which was mine; the fulfilment was left to others.

The garden, the courtyard, and the adjacent sylvan squares give release to a country Friend immured for so many hours within the portals of Friends House. The Yearly Meeting Epistle, in 1975, recorded this: 'We have walked under the sunlit green of city trees. We have heard children playing in the courtyard. A blackbird has sung constantly throughout our words and silence'. But they do more. During the decade or so of change

37

heralded by the 1965 Church Government Revision Committee's report *New Life from Old Roots*, some members of Friends House staff, notably Arthur White, Edward Milligan, Walter Martin, and later Geoffrey Bowes, spent many lunchtime breaks walking in the environs of Friends House and sharing ideas for the integration of Friends House staff, for a more satisfactory committee structure, for financial arrangements which would reflect the unity of all our work. It was rumoured that these peregrinations were to avoid the possibility of being bugged in the Recording Clerk's Office! An unworthy thought, but did we gain more than privacy from the catalpa (an Indian bean tree) and the rhododendrons in St George's gardens, from the tulips and laburnum trees in Tavistock Square, and from the periwinkle and the standard roses in Gordon Square?

One happy conjunction of events is that the Royal Horticultural Society Chelsea Flower Show comes in the week when Yearly Meeting begins— preparation indeed! Among all else to be prepared for Yearly Meeting are the flowers on the platform and on the Clerks' table in the Large Meeting House. It is long years since the Society's accountant rose early and visited nearby Covent Garden to return with boxes of blooms and festooned with foliage. In some recent years, we have achieved lesser glories by a kind of DIY process, and Edward Milligan has made light of the difficulties of bearing beech branches from Reading, via Paddington and Euston Square, as if Birnam Wood had come to Dunsinane.

Residential Yearly Meetings can afford opportunities to visit fresh fields and pastures new—Warwick 1984 provided Hidcote, Exeter (in 1986) will offer the riches of Knightshayes and Cotehele, Trelissick and Trewithen . . . And not only in Great Britain . . . or only public gardens, but those of individual Friends. I can remember—perhaps I should not be particular—but occasional packets of seeds in the morning post in the Recording Clerk's Office make wonderful reminders. On one occasion when the Yearly Meeting Agenda Committee was meeting in Ealing we took an afternoon off to visit Kew Gardens. The then Yearly Meeting Clerk was heard to comment 'I did not know that Geoffrey Bowes was so knowledgeable about plants'. Trust Arthur White to make a typical rejoinder: 'Just you watch him. He goes ahead and looks at the labels'. On reflection, not such a bad thing for any kind of clerk to do. I recall the advice in 'General Counsel on Church Affairs', *Church Government*, §726: 'Check beforehand all facts which may be in question, so as to avoid plunging the whole meeting into fruitless and time-wasting speculation'.

'The Librarian works closely with the Recording Clerk's Office . . .' (job description for the Librarian). There was an occasion when, the flowers for the Clerks' table at Meeting for Sufferings having been over-looked, the Librarian made a selection of flowers from the garden and the

Recording Clerk arranged them. Is it too fanciful to think that simple act symptomatic of our close collaboration as we are 'involved in the Society's day to day administration'? Edward Milligan might well say with George Herbert: 'I made a posy while the day ran by'. Rarely a day passes without such offerings, a comment on a problem or on people gleaned from the wide field of his unrivalled communications network, or a response to a chance remark, or a sudden request for a note on when last the Yearly Meeting considered this or that. These arrive on scraps of paper typed hurriedly on the red ribbon. A knowledgeable Friend once said 'Ted in red is always worth reading'.

There are other more weighty matters subject for a more carefully selected, more formal bouquet. A paper on Friends' marriage procedure, a history of the Yearly Meeting Epistle, a note on the work of the last Book of Discipline Revision Committee perhaps. Such bouquets need time to choose, to gather, to select, to discard and select afresh.

> My hand was next to them, and then my heart:
> I took, without more thinking, in good part
> Time's gentle admonition . . .

The more impatient admonition of the Recording Clerk working to a particular deadline may well have been less welcome!

There are times when

> Within my head, aches the perpetual winter
> Of this violent time, where pleasures freeze.

Less dramatic, but no less real, there are occasions (dare one admit it?) when one prepares for a committee feeling more the barrenness of winter than summer's fecundity. Then the Library can supply solace for a Recording Clerk who sees 'the garden, falsified by snow'. Ten minutes with the flower illustrations in *Woodland Plants*, by Heather and Robin Tanner, with Sidney Parkinson's work as artist of Cook's *Endeavour* voyage, or Will Fox and M.E.Norwood Young's *Food from the Veld: Edible Wild Plants of Southern Africa* can, to coin a phrase, refresh those parts other books cannot reach.

Enough; there is a rose called the Rambling Rector—perhaps there should be one called the Rambling Recording Clerk.

LOCAL VARIATIONS IN QUAKER MEETING HOUSES

by David M. Butler

When travelling in unfamiliar places there is a pleasure to be had from recognising the local Quaker meeting house, a pleasure which I first enjoyed in the company of E.H.M. We think we know what we shall find: 'typical of the district' perhaps, or 'what we would expect at that period'. Yet on looking more carefully we see that each one has its own distinctive character. This is not just a matter of building materials and methods, for Friends built pretty much as the man next door; it has to do with the presence and arrangement of peculiarly Quaker features. Friends in different periods and places built their new meeting house to suit themselves, aware of how their old one was inadequate and with knowledge of what both neighbouring and more distant meetings had done. In the notes which follow a few of these local Quaker distinctions are described, and some thought given to the circumstances which led to them, and to their effect.

The notes are based on dated surveys (many the work of good friends having similar interests) of some four hundred meeting houses, out of about one thousand places built or bought for Quaker worship during the life of London Yearly Meeting. When these are grouped by historical counties (which were the basis of Quaker boundaries) and by chronological periods from 1650 to 1950 (after which date the traditional types

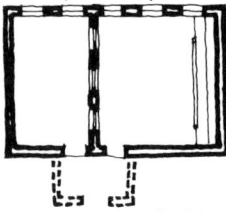

Beckfoot

Kendal

Brigflatts

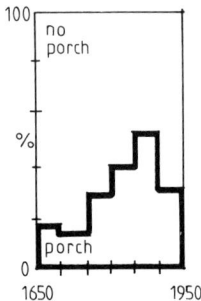

were little used) comparisons may be made and trends discerned. Not that the comparisons are absolutely clear-cut, for always a few examples stray in from other places and periods, and relatively little is recorded from some counties. All the same, from what material is available one may at least put forward a working hypothesis on Friends' attitude to, for instance, placing a porch around their meeting house door.

This might seem a poor example to choose, for forthright Quakers would have been expected to build a porch only where one was needed: where the entrance was exposed to the weather or the building set in a region of harsher climate, and not in milder places. Yet the reality was otherwise, as some examples may show.

The meeting house at Beckfoot was built in 1745 with the doors (but not the windows) facing the Cumberland coast, and with no porch. A sketch made a century later[1] showed it still so: not until the gales of a hundred and forty winters had blown in was one built. At Kendal in 1816 the rebuilding committee asked their architect to supply plans for porches, but not until the meeting house was almost finished; thus a porch was not to be expected then even for a really substantial and comfortable town meeting house. The contrast is more marked when it is remembered that the earliest meeting houses near Kendal, including Brigflatts (1675) and Height (1677), were built with large and useful porches. Thus the local precedent existed, it may seem to us that the need existed, yet many meeting houses particularly in the north and west were not provided with the improvement in comfort which a porch offered at such slight expense.

The chart shows how slowly porches came to be accepted, rising from one in five to a maximum of one porch to two meeting houses late in the nineteenth century, and rather surprisingly falling away in our own period. The later growth in number of porches was centred on south-east England, with its relatively mild climate. In Quaker terms London and Middlesex Quarterly Meeting was an area of particular strength and unity, and furthermore was better served than

42

elsewhere by visits from Friends travelling in the ministry; thus the exchange of news and ideas was rapid and thorough. The increase commenced c.1800 in and immediately around London, and reached counties a stage further out later in the century. Clearly quite different attitudes prevailed in the south east, where urban prosperity and fashion were among the factors relevant to the large number of porches.

The porch has been discussed simply as an illustration and we now turn to more essential considerations. Most meeting houses fall into one of two types, one of which may be described as *cottage*, the other as *chapel*. The former was naturally the earlier and in the first hundred years accounted for perhaps 90% of all meeting houses, in the second hundred 60%, and in the third only 35%. During the transitional period Derbyshire, Somerset, and the North Riding appear to have been reluctant to change while London (though not the counties immediately around) was well in the forefront of the chapel style. The last century shows Somerset again, with Westmorland and Essex, keeping to the cottage when chapels were to be expected.

Interestingly Friends made very little use of the elements of the typical early nonconformist meeting house. This had two doors in a symmetrical long wall and a pulpit in the centre of (usually) the opposite wall, with an upper gallery or loft on two or three sides. The whole interior was fitted out with box-pews, the two doors following from the need to have a large centre block of pews directly in front of the pulpit. Such buildings were erected over a long period of time throughout the country and so were well known to Friends. The rate and distribution of the change from this pattern to the chapel form will make an interesting comparison with the corresponding change in Quaker meeting houses when sufficient data becomes available.

Some of the reasons for the change of plan type are not far to find: having to do with up-dating the image of a meeting house which had once really been a cottage, the need to fit into closely built urban areas, the example set by chapels of other denominations, perhaps

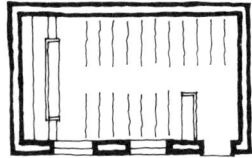

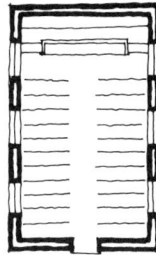

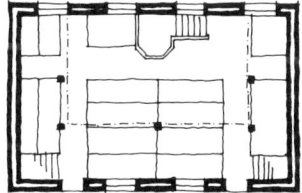

even the expectations of Friends recently joined from other churches. Reasons are not always so easy to find for the many variations of the basic plans which found favour in one small period or part of the country. Here are a few examples.

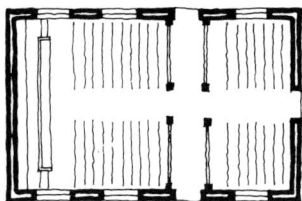

Cornish Friends made use of a handsome form of meeting house, putting up at least four during a fifteen year period early in the last century. They were large granite boxes up to 60 by 30 feet, with a central passage between two sets of large sash shutters, and had three entrance doors. The thoroughfares defined by the doors were paved with stone flags and the quarters for seats boarded. The variety and ease of access was unusual, nevertheless the first of the kind at Redruth in 1814 must have been found to answer well or it would not have been repeated so literally elsewhere in the county. The geographical and cultural isolation of Cornwall could have led Friends on their very independent course.

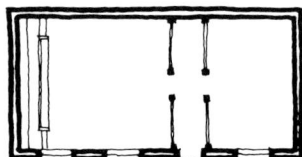

The other type of meeting house which has a central passage between two sets of shutters is not so closely defined geographically but appears predominantly in the North Riding where at least seven were built between about 1770 and 1840, with nearly as many in Essex. Its precursors were in Lancashire north of the Sands where Height (1677) and Swarthmoor (1688) were both so altered by the addition of a second timber partition not long after they were built. The arrangement was developed by a nineteenth-century York Friend, William Alexander, in his book *Observations on the Construction . . . of Meeting Houses*,[2] though it is doubtful whether more than two or three were built to his very precisely-defined scheme.

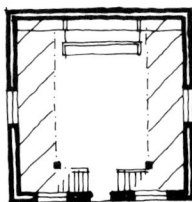

A form of meeting house found very frequently in Norfolk is attractive for its regularity, small scale, and the way the interior is furnished. Typically it is nearly square, with a hipped roof, has a small ministers' stand on the wall opposite the door, and a narrow loft along each side wall reached by steps just inside the door. These Georgian red brick and pantile buildings with large sash windows and white-painted timber pediment over the door have atmosphere and style. What they do not have however is the separate chamber for women's business meetings, and given that Quakers in Norfolk did not need one they show what can be done when one of the customary requirements is removed. The general need for a dividing screen makes an important contribution to the character of our meeting houses, and these Norfolk buildings are perhaps the less Quakerly for its absence. They represent in fact the nearest Quaker equivalent to the old nonconformist plan described earlier.

While the chapel plan showed its strength more in the south of England one particular development is characteristic of towns in Cumberland and Westmorland. It faces, and solves, the problem of combining large seating capacity with the need to divide into two chambers on occasions. The more usual solution of placing them end to end tended to excessive length. Here in Cumberland the two chambers, two self-contained meeting houses in fact, were placed side by side and separated by a wall of large timber panels drawn up and down by winch (and whose design shows interesting technical innovation). Most had a connecting lobby; a few opened straight into the fresh air. Its first appearance was at Whitehaven in 1725 followed (with improvements) at Carlisle, Kendal, Wigton and Cockermouth; all the large meeting houses in the area, in fact. No doubt it was through the Pease family connection with Kendal that the same type was adopted in Darlington in 1846, one of the largest meeting houses built in this country, and the same pattern was used very effectively on a diminutive scale at Wisbech in 1854. William Alexander developed this plan too in his book[3] and at some length, but in a way which was not likely to be used.

Two other forms of town meeting house stand out. One was developed in London in the mid nineteenth-century and incorporated substantial side rooms (classrooms or cloakrooms) linked by a colonnade in front of the meeting room, thus giving a street façade a good deal wider and potentially more interesting than the average meeting house could offer. Examples are at Stoke Newington (1828) and Peckham (1826): they

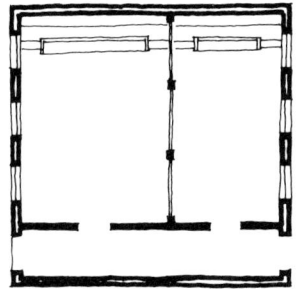

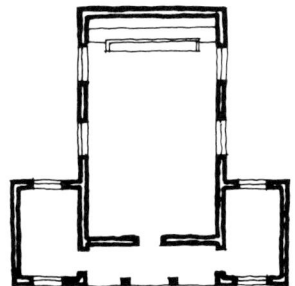

relate closely to the development of outlying villages into suburbs of the city, which in Stoke Newington began about 1820.

The second was the work of the Quaker architect Hubert Lidbetter (1885-1966). It was the result of a deliberate fresh approach to meeting house design, combining the need for compact seating for either small or large gatherings with good access and lines of vision. Coupled with these more traditional virtues was the provision of much larger lobbies than before to answer the wishes of twentieth-century Friends. It took the form of a high square room with lobbies around three sides and lofts above them. Three were built in this pattern, Friends House in 1930, Bull Street Birmingham in 1933 and Liverpool 1948. All were thus for large meetings in city centres, for which there is now not so much demand.

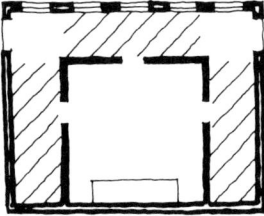

Even the foundation of a Friends School can be shown to have an influence upon the design of the local meeting house. It led usually to rebuilding, thence through the influence of the perhaps national rather than local school committee to the choice of a plan unconnected with local tradition. Thus at Sibford a small old country meeting house was replaced in 1864 with a slightly reduced version of the nineteenth-century London plan. On the other hand at Wigton when school and meeting came to agree that the old thatched cottage would no longer do, the school architect, a man from outside the area, did in fact adopt and develop the local Cumberland plan to good effect.

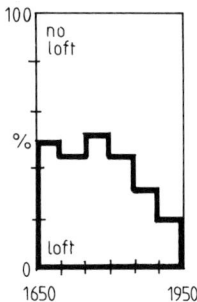

Most meeting house types were capable of incorporating an upper public gallery or loft, and local tradition might be expected to affect its distribution. In fact the indistinct pattern of distribution and apparently random changes in popularity suggest that other influences must have prevailed. The likelihood of a loft being built was never better than about 50% and has declined to about 20% in our own time. It appeared little in the counties around London and was hardly ever found in Essex, while Friends in the south-west made much greater use of it.

Of the internal furnishings of a meeting house the

ministers' stand may very effectively be analysed. Considered most simply it comes in three types: where the raised seat occupies only the centre part of the back wall, where it spans the full width of the wall, and where there is no raised seat but only a platform.

The first type started off well, specially in Norfolk and the Cotswolds, but declined fairly rapidly. It was perhaps better suited to the more domestic scale of meeting house and to the smaller meeting which had little expectation of a powerful presence of Friends sitting facing. Herein lay a factor in its decline, for formal eldership, which needed greater seating capacity, was a late development in church government and made itself felt only from the mid eighteenth-century.[4] The connection with eldership appeared again in the slight resurgence of the small stand when it reflected the declining importance of the elders' bench over a century later. It led in places to the use instead of a simple platform, particularly where mission work was strong.

One of the sub-species of the central stand is however largely confined to Yorkshire where at least eight examples are known, the earliest of 1689. It incorporates a seat occupying both front corners of the room beside the stand, raised a step above the floor and enclosed by a low panelled screen. It gives the side seats greater prominence than they would otherwise command, half way between the ministers and the body of the meeting. The pattern seems to find an echo in smaller Welsh chapels of some two centuries later where seats for elders are grouped around the pulpit.

An interesting version of the ministers' stand was built in the area of Pardshaw meeting from 1710 to 1740, and consisted of a raised seat on each side of a central fireplace.[5] This arrangement was rather more effective for warming than for ministry: at that time heating the main meeting room was not thought necessary, and perhaps for this reason the arrangement never spread outside Cumberland. It appeared to originate in a cottage altered to make a meeting house, where the facing benches were set either side of the hearth.

What has been discussed so far is no more than an

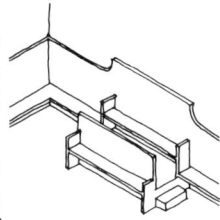

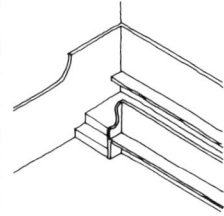

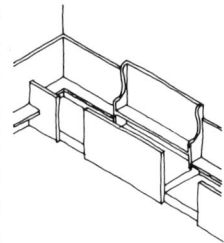

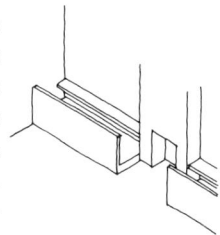

appetizer. It scarcely touches on the possibilities opened up by this approach to the study of our past. When the date and location, the types and the features of meeting houses are analysed in depth, connections will be made for example with the regional history and geography and agricultural practice, population changes and prosperity, dissent and establishment. Their combined study should enlarge our understanding of Quaker history by bringing out the often hidden local relationships between the meeting and the world outside. It should also reveal more of the way meeting houses were made and used, and thereby help us to see further into the minds of early Friends not only through the way they wrote and spoke (for here we have gone some way) but as they realised their thoughts in bricks and mortar.

NOTES

[1] Friends House Library, Gibson MSS, vol. 6, p. 241.
[2] (York, 1820), plate 4.
[3] *Ibid.*, plate 5.
[4] W.C.Braithwaite, *Second Period of Quakerism* (1919), p. 543.
[5] D.M.Butler, *Quaker Meeting Houses of the Lake Counties* (1978), pp. ix-xi.

QUAKERS AND MUGGLETONIANS IN SEVENTEENTH-CENTURY IRELAND

by Kenneth L.Carroll

Revolutionary England produced a tremendous spectrum of religious development, creating among others such diverse movements as Quakers, Fifth Monarchists, Muggletonians, Seekers, and Ranters. Of all these groups only two—Quakerism and Muggletonianism—lasted into the twentieth century. As far as is known, the last Muggletonian died in 1979, thereby (along with the discovery of the great Muggletonian archives that had been in his possession) inspiring a new interest in and study of that religious body. The most significant work thus far to have come out of this renewed concern with this previously obscure sect has been *The World of the Muggletonians*.[1]

The Muggletonians stem from the work of John Reeve and his cousin Lodowick Muggleton, who appeared as 'prophets' in 1652, proclaiming that they were the 'last two witnesses' promised in Revelation 11.3. The movement took its name from Muggleton (1609-98), who outlived Reeve (1608-58), thus becoming the more significant of the two. Never very large, the Muggletonian body was numbered in the hundreds,[2] whereas Quakerism which began at roughly the same time soon reached into the thousands and then into the tens of thousands.

England was the main scene of the Muggletonians, although in the 1670s they made some small inroads into Ireland where the radical

Puritanism of many members of the ex-New Model Army provided fertile ground for their growth,[3] just as it had earlier for the spread of Quakerism throughout the Cromwellian Army in Ireland.[4] One of the more outstanding officers of the New Model Army who flirted with Quakerism but never really became convinced of Quaker principles was Colonel Robert Phayre [Phaire], once governor of Cork. He was first attracted to Friends by the 1655 preaching of Francis Howgill,[5] and attended meetings for a time but never really embraced Quakerism (as shown by the letter from Robert Story to Phayre).[6] From flirting with Quakerism Phayre (1619?-82) moved on to the Ranters and finally became a Muggletonian—becoming the most important one in Ireland.[7]

Two centres of Muggletonianism developed in Ireland—one in Cork and the other in Dublin.[8] In Cork a number of Quakers were drawn into the Muggletonian camp, but there is no evidence that this same thing happened in Dublin.[9] It would appear that Colonel Phayre was the initial leader in the growth of the Cork Muggletonian movement. Phayre first met Muggleton in London in 1661, received his first letter from Muggleton in 1670, and also circulated the writings of Reeve and Muggleton.[10] Soon Dr Joseph Moss was drawn into the circle, followed by George Rogers (neither of whom seem to have been Quakers).[11]

The first significant Quaker loss to the Muggletonians was George Gamble, a Cork merchant who had been an active Friend for a number of years. He had suffered imprisonment on three or four occasions from 1662 to 1668 when arrested for attending a meeting for worship.[12] In 1669, 1670, and 1671 there were four occasions when some of his goods were seized when he refused to pay for the maintenance of the priest.[13] George Gamble, who seems to have been doubly connected to Colonel Phayre by marriage,[14] was still in good standing with Friends in early 1671 when the last case of his suffering was recorded by Irish Friends.[15] When he withdrew from Friends, Cork Quakers actually sought Gamble's 'recovery' to Quakerism 'untill he slighted their Service of Love, and they found theire spirits withdrawn from him as a person left without hope'.[16]

The exact date of George Gamble's defection from Quakerism is uncertain, but it appears to have begun in late 1671 or early 1672. A letter from Muggleton to Gamble, dated March 6, 1672[3], notes that some time earlier Gamble had met with Muggleton in London (perhaps as a result of a growing interest in Muggleton's doctrines, as made known to him by his 'kinsman' Colonel Phayre). Following this visit to London Gamble had returned to Ireland and for a time was so sick that he appeared 'like to die' but finally had written a letter to Muggleton on February 14, 1672[3] in which he had reported his improving health. Muggleton responded to this news of Gamble's illness by writing:

The Quakers would have been glad in their hearts if you had been dead indeed; because they might have had occasion to ground a belief, that God's judgments did follow you *so suddenly after you forsook the Quakers principles,* and did cleave to Muggleton's doctrine, because several of the Quakers have died in a little time after they were damned by me: so they would willingly have some to die that fall from them; looking upon it as a curse upon them for falling away from their principles.[17]

Other Cork Quakers who defected to Muggletonianism in the 1670s were George Webber, Henry Flaggator, and Andrew Vivers. Webber, who had suffered for his Quaker faith in 1663, 1666, and 1670,[18] was remembered by Cork Friends as one who had 'wittnessed a measure of the power and life of truth and was often constrained in meetings to beare testimony thereto: exhorting and Warning others to be faithful to the same, very often extolling the way of truth calling it the blessed way & blessed truth, saying there was no other'.[19] Webber, who had been a close friend of George Gamble, felt a concern to draw Gamble back to Friends after the meeting had finally given up its efforts to retrieve him. In his frequent visits with Gamble, Webber's 'own understanding became vailed [so that he] lost his tendernesse to truth, & began little by little to leave off meetings, & more & more to accompany those people who had set themselves above it and delighted in liberty & pleasure'. Cork Friends, aware of the 'Danger attending the said G. Webber, did in the wisdome of God lay it before him: and many & often were the tender vissitations of friends for his recovery, which he slighted haveing drunk in that wrong spirit which wrought misteriously against the truth and so he became numn'd and stupid in his senses (as to the sense of truth)'.[20]

Henry Flaggator[21] and Andrew Vivers[22] likewise were drawn into the Muggletonian camp. When Friends admonished them, they rejected this advice—requesting that they be left 'to their liberty and freedom (as they called it) untill such time it was too mannifest, their liberty wrought them into great bondage; and so they quite departed from Meetings'.[23]

It was probably Gamble's apostasy, followed by that of these other members of the meeting, that led Cork Friends to identify Muggletonian principles and testify against him. When the Cork General Meeting [Munster Provincial Meeting] wrote to the National Meeting about these principles, the answer came back from the larger body that,

> friends here doe unanimously detest and deny [Muggleton's principles], and are glad to finde friends att Corke, Concerned to beare their testimony against them, and that Spiritt and to Read & Publish

the Same in their Gen[e]rall Meeting att Corke and Record their said Testimony against the said Spirritt & Principles in their Province book.[24]

Munster Province Meeting drew up a list of the errors of John Reeve and Lodowick Muggleton, especially attacking their claims that they were the 'last two witnesses of the spirit', that Muggleton was the only interpreter of the Bible, that Muggleton was the only judge of what becomes of men and women after death, that Muggleton had the power of blessing and cursing 'and that unrevoakably to all Eternity', and that Muggleton knew 'more of spirituall things than ever [any] prophet or Apostle did since the beginning of the world'.[25] Friends then proceeded to pick out a number of other 'errors' found in Muggletonian books, including the claim that Elias [Elijah] had been exalted to the 'throne of glory' for a moment to represent God the Father when 'God became a child' and that 'it was Elias that fil[le]d the lord Jesus with those great revelations of his former glory that he possessed in the heavens when he was the imortall father, and it was Elias that spoak those words from heaven saying this is my beloved sone, etc'.[26]

The fact that a handful of Cork Quakers had been drawn to the Muggletonian position led to a 'false rumour . . . spread abroad' that a much larger body of Cork Friends had 'received the doctrines & principles of the afores[ai]d Reve & Muggleton, whereby some honest hearted may seem to stumble or startle.' Thus, twenty-six Friends [27] (many of whom were rumoured to have turned to Muggletonian views), at a General Meeting for the Province of Munster held in Cork on the 17th of the 4 Month [June] 1673, testified against the rival movement:

> [We] have very seriously and in the councell of god Weighed and considered the Principles and doctrines of the aforesaid Reve and Muggleton, and the spirit from whence they flow. And doe in the name & Authority of the holy spirit of truth Judge and condemne that spirit as a spirit of errour and Blasphamie sprung from the bottomless pitt of darkness, and high presumption. And by this our Testimony doe deny & detest the same, as neither fitt to touch, tast[e] nor handle of. Warning and admonishing all people in the feare and dread of the Lord God of heaven and Earth, both to turn from it and avoyd it.[28]

Less than a month later, on 11 July 1673, Dr Joseph Moss of Cork wrote to Lodowick Muggleton in London sending him a copy of this Quaker 'testimony' against the Muggletonian principles, saying 'I thought it not amiss to acquaint you with the Transactions, Testimony, & Rage of the

Serpents seed here in these part, who like roreing [roaring] Lions wander up & down seeking whom they may devour, having given their disciples that oath of Aligience in manner, though not in forme'.[29]

On 11 August 1673, Muggleton responded to this Cork Quaker Testimony, pronouncing the twenty-six Cork Quakers 'cursed and damned, in their souls and bodies, from the presence of God, elect men and angels, to eternity'. Thus they took their place with many other Friends cursed by 'the prophet Muggleton', including George Fox, Edward Burrough, Elizabeth Hooton, Francis Howgill, Thomas Loe, William Penn, and Thomas Taylor.[30] Muggleton, who is quoted as saying that cursing people did him more good 'than if a Man had given him Forty Shillings',[31] on one occasion claims to have damned 'hundreds', while elsewhere he brags that he and Reeve had cursed 'near upon a thousand' in a ten-year period.[32] When this letter cursing the Cork Quakers was later published in *Spiritual Epistles* (1755) a number of the names were greatly mis-spelled and one of them Thomas Campion (which Moss had turned into Timothy Weymouth) became Timothy *Thohoymouth*.[33] One sometimes wonders just who was being cursed and how effective it was!

One of the contributing factors to the Cork attack on Muggleton's principles was the appearance of William Penn's *The New Witnesses Proved Old Hereticks* in 1672, in which Penn (who had strong connections with Cork Quakerism) vigorously attacks Muggleton's teachings[34] as well as rejecting Muggleton's claim that his cursing of Thomas Loe (shortly after Loe's own 1668 attack on Muggleton) was responsible for bringing on Loe's death.[35] Loe, who has been called the 'Apostle to Ireland', had strong Cork ties, and it was in Cork that Loe had converted Penn to Quakerism c.1666. Penn ordered two dozen copies of this tract to be sent to Ireland.[36] Probably Penn's work, as well as the increasing Irish Quaker awareness of what was happening, led to the end—at least temporarily—of slippage to the Muggletonians.

Why had these Friends left Quakerism for Muggletonianism? No final answer can be given, for we have no relevant materials to examine. Yet one is tempted to suggest a number of possible motives or factors which combined to produce this result. Some individuals, such as George Gamble, seem to have been truly convinced of the validity of Muggleton's 'Commission'. Also, to some degree, knowing that one is of the 'elect' or 'blessed' produces a certain sense of security (as well as the pride that necessarily goes with that 'knowledge'). In addition, Muggletonianism allowed individuals (some of whom had already suffered heavily as Quakers) to escape persecution. No longer did they have to meet at specific times, for regular meetings were not a Muggletonian requirement. They could now pay tithes and thereby escape the distraining of goods which many had earlier suffered. Some even put in appearances at the established church in order to avoid fines which came from non-attendance. Thus, they were given a way to side-step suffering and persecution and feel truly 'spiritual' at the same time (much as John Perrot had helped Virginia Quakers escape persecution by putting aside the *form* of meeting for worship at a regular time and yet feel that they were more 'religious' or 'spiritual' than those who insisted on meeting at a pre-arranged time).[37] Muggletonianism was, in a sense, a very *easy* religion, so that John Gratton (who became a Quaker in 1674 after earlier Muggletonian and Baptist affiliations) wrote that the Muggletonians 'had no worship at all, nor when we met together . . . we were not for either waiting upon God or for any other Exercise at all of either Preaching, Praying, or Reading holy Scriptures: No we had no more to do, but to believe Muggleton and be saved'.[38]

There appears to have been some further slight defection of Cork Quakers to the Muggletonian movement about 1681. In that year Lodowick Muggleton wrote to Charles Yeeles, Thomas Millerd, and John White of Cork, saying 'I perceive *some* of you have been Quakers'.[39] It is known that White had been a Quaker,[40] but there is some question about the other two. Given Muggleton's use of 'some of you', it would be wrong to follow unquestioningly Reay's view that all three had been Quakers.[41]

It was this threat of further slippage from Quakerism to Muggletonianism that produced the 1681 'testimony and record' concerning Webber, Flaggator, and Vivers, 'all of the cittie of Cork, who professed the Lord's truth and for a time were Zealous therein, but not keeping in the continuance of that lowly principle which at first convinced them they declined meetings, seperated themselves from god's people, and dyed out of the faith and unity of the Gospel'. Webber, Cork Friends recorded, 'did not long after [his rejection of Friends] enjoy his health; but was vissitted with sickness and lingering distemper of which he never recovered but dyed in that state of apostacie from truth'.[42] Concerning Flaggator, it was noted that after he set aside meetings, he did not enjoy 'himself Long before sickness & distemper of body came on him which held him no little time, nor without very torturing paines as have been reported by some that vissitted him in his sickness: of which sickness he also dyed'.[43] Andrew Vivers, they reported, had not long left the Society of Friends when

> hee became vaine and Loose in his conversation, and kept bad company: p[ar]ticulerly haunted another man's Wife of Ill Fame and being gone behind hand in the World he went to service to the aforementioned George Gamble, where the lord vissitted him with a very terrible sickness: in which he was like a man distracted by the

violence thereof: crying out for water or something to cool his tongue. And as the hand of the Lord was heavie upon him in his sickness, soe his countenance looked very ghastly & woefull to the beholders;—raveing and spending himselfe untill he dyed. And after death his vissage was sayd to be more ghastly than others.[44]

George Gamble died in 1682, some years after Webber, Flaggator, and Vivers. A later hand has added, at the end of the above 1681 'testimony and record', the notation 'As for the said Geo. Gamble, tho' he lived some years after these three men He dyed in apostacy and hardness of heart against the truth'.[45] With the death of Gamble and Phayre, both in 1682, the life seems to have gone out of the Cork Muggletonian group, so that no longer did it hold much attraction for Quakers or others. Slowly the numbers declined, so that by 1800 only one Muggletonian was to be found in all Ireland. Irish Quaker concern over the Muggletonian threat had ceased even before the end of the seventeenth century, for the 'threat' itself had ceased to exist.

NOTES

[1] Christopher Hill, Barry Reay, and William Lamont, *The World of the Muggletonians* (London, 1983).
[2] *Ibid.*, p. 55.
[3] *Ibid.*, pp. 55-56.
[4] Kenneth L.Carroll, 'Quakerism and the Cromwellian Army in Ireland,' *Journal of the Friends Historical Society*, 51 (1976-82), 135-54.
[5] *Ibid.*, 51, 141-42.
[6] Swarthmore MSS VI, 27 (Tr. VII, 527). This letter from Story to Phayre is undated. Cf. Swarthmore MSS VI, 37 (Tr. VII, 556) where Francis Howgill writes (in 1656) 'I wrote lately to Coll: Phaire plainely.' Also see William C.Braithwaite (second edition, revised by Henry J.Cadbury), *The Beginnings of Quakerism* (Cambridge, 1955), pp. 214, 216, 219.
[7] Hill, Reay, and Lamont, *op. cit.*, p. 35, say that Phayre was the local leader of the Muggletonians, receiving correspondence, organising infrequent local meetings, and selling Muggletonian tracts.
[8] *Ibid.*, p. 55.
[9] There are clear references to Muggleton and his followers in Cork Quaker records but not in the Dublin ones (where references to Ranters does not seem to refer to Muggletonians, although the title was sometimes applied to them).
[10] 'Phayre, Robert', *Dictionary of National Biography* (London, 1896), XLV, 142-43.
[11] Alexander Delemaine, *A Volume of Spiritual Epistles: Being the Copies of Several Letters Written by the two last Prophets and Messengers of God, John Reeve and Lodowicke Muggleton* (London, 1755), p. 253.
[12] National Sufferings, I (1655-93), 34, 49. This manuscript volume, now numbered YM Gl, is found in the Friends Historical Library, Eustance Street, Dublin. Cf. Joseph Besse, *A Collection of the Sufferings of the People Called Quakers* (London, 1753), II, 472, 475, 476.
[13] National Sufferings, I, 58, 64, 78; Besse, *op. cit.*, II, 477.

[14] Colonel Phayre's first wife is thought to have been a Gamble, while George Gamble's third (?) wife was Phayre's daughter—cf. *DNB*, XLV, 143. Gamble by his first (?) wife had a daughter Sarah who married William Fennell at Cork Meeting in 1675. Gamble then married Jane Gore in a meeting of Limerick in 1668. The date of his marriage to Mary Phayre is unknown.

[15] National Sufferings, I, 78.

[16] Cork Testimonies of Disunity and Epistles (MMIII, Fl), p. 4. This information is found in the middle of the testimony concerning George Webber. This volume is hereafter referred to as Cork Testimonies and is found in Friends Historical Library, Dublin.

[17] *Spiritual Epistles*, pp. 93-96. Italics added.

[18] Besse, *Sufferings*, II, 473, 475, 477.

[19] Cork Testimonies, p. 4.

[20] *Ibid.*, p. 4.

[21] Henry Flaggator (Flaggeter, etc.) had a wife Elizabeth, to whom Muggleton wrote on several occasions, and a number of children.

[22] Andrew Vivers, formerly of Banbury in Oxfordshire, settled in Cork sometime before his 1669 marriage to the widow Elizabeth Pike. His relationship to Edward Vivers, well-known Banbury Friend, is uncertain.

[23] Cork Testimonies, pp. 4-5.

[24] National Meeting Proceedings (½YM Al), p. 15, dated 5th of 3rd Month (May), 1673. This manuscript volume is found in Friends Historical Library, Dublin.

[25] Cork Testimonies, pp. 1-2.

[26] *Ibid.*, p. 2.

[27] *Ibid.*, p. 3. Those who signed this testimony were William Morris, William Edmondson, Francis Rogers, Robert Sandham, Phillip Dymond, William Edwards, John Fennell, Thomas Wight, John Gossage, Thomas Wheedon, Thomas Gettos, Thomas Campion, Richard Berry, John Burnyatt [Burnyeat], George Patteson, James Dowlen, William End, Christopher Pennock, Thomas Alley, Jasper Tregos, John Haman, Daniel Savery, Arthur Johnson, Walter Phillips, William Hawkins, and George Neynoe.

[28] *Ibid.*, p. 3.

[29] Letter from Jos[eph] Moss, Cork, to Lodowick Muggleton, dated 11 July 1673, (found in Muggleton Manuscripts No. 60168, British Library, London). Moss's list of the Quaker signers substitutes the name of Timothy Wheymouth for that of Thomas Campion. There are some minor differences in the spelling of several other names.

[30] *Spiritual Epistles*, pp. 84, 85, 91.

[31] Hill, Reay, and Lamont, *op. cit.*, p. 29.

[32] *Ibid.*, p. 29. Cf. p. 75 where Christopher Hill reports that Muggleton 'damned 103 persons, nearly half of whom were Quakers'. Although I was not able to review all the relevant Muggletonian manuscripts (because the room in which they are housed was suddenly closed in July 1984 to remove asbestos from the walls), I have thus far identified 54 Quakers whom he cursed.

[33] *Spiritual Epistles*, p. 79. Among the errors are Fossage for Gossage, Burngate for Burnyatt (Burnyeat), Penricke for Pennock, Negno for Neyno, and Treyos for Tregos.

[34] William Penn, *The New Witnesses Proved Old Hereticks* (London, 1672), pp. 2-62.

[35] *Ibid.*, p. 40.

[36] Mary Maples Dunn and Richard S. Dunn, eds., *The Papers of William Penn* (University of Pennsylvania Press, 1981), I, 87, 88, 599.

[37] Kenneth L. Carroll, *John Perrot, Early Quaker Schismatic* (London, 1971), pp. 75, 99-102.

[38] John Gratton, *A Journal of the Life of that Ancient Servant of Christ, John Gratton* (London, 1720), pp. 24-25.

[39] *Spiritual Epistles*, p. 385. Italics added.
[40] Besse, *Sufferings*, II, 472, 478.
[41] Hill, Reay, and Lamont, *op. cit.*, p 47.
[42] Cork Testimonies, p. 4.
[43] *Ibid.*, p. 5.
[44] *Ibid.*, p. 5.
[45] *Ibid.*, p. 5.

WOUNDED HEALERS: MINISTRY AND PASTORAL CARE IN A BROKEN WORLD

by Jo Farrow

All of us are wounded healers
  Henri Nouwen[1]

Many people were shocked when they saw him
he was so disfigured that he hardly looked human . . .
Who could have seen the Lord's hand in this . . .
He had no dignity or beauty
to make us take notice of him . . .
We despised and rejected him,
he endured suffering and pain
No one would even look at him—
we ignored him as if he were nothing.
But he endured the suffering that should have been ours
the pain that we should have borne . . .
We are healed by the punishment he suffered,
made whole by the blows he received.
  Isaiah 52, 14, and 53, 1b-4a[2]

There is nothing new about the experience of living in a dislocated world. The feelings of pain, vulnerability and anxiety which we suffer as we become sharply aware of the violence and disorder in our present situation are part of the common experience of humankind. Nor are we alone in longing for a different order of things or in feeling the pain so over-whelmingly that at times we hope for some kind of miraculous interven-tion, even though we know that in a world in which human beings are free to remain unaware and blind to reality there will always be the possibility of great evil. One of the most salutary lessons in our current situation is that the craving for a strong and superhuman leader, who will solve our predicament by doing the massive work of salvage and rehabilitation for us, continues to play a large part in human expectations. These hopes and longings are part of the age-old dream of humanity and expressed with poignancy in every religious tradition either in terms of a messianic saviour, or a spiritual leader who will point the way to enlightenment and liberty. The charismatic figures we select to embody our dream of libera-tion are very often those 'larger than life' human beings whose heroic achievements tower above us like Himalayan peaks. Friends are not immune to temptations of power, the desire that our spiritual trail-blazers shall do it successfully and with proper acknowledgment and publicity. Nor are we free of that form of nostalgia which prompts us to look back to a golden age when Friends were cast in more heroic mould and blessed with visions clearer than our own. We project onto them the virtues and breadth of vision which we fail to recognise in our contemporaries, and are angry and disheartened if some rather less biased historian uncovers the clay feet of our idols and shows us their flawed or incomplete humanity.

Yet we create the seeds of our own paralysis when we idolise what is not ultimate, and cheat ourselves out of our birthright. For the truth is that when we gild the men and women of earlier ages with the veneer of some kind of superhumanity, removing all traces of their neuroses and frailty, they have ceased to be of any real use to us except as carefully preserved exhibits in a museum stuffed with our own illusions. George Fox strug-gling with depression is more reassuring to me as a human being learning to trust my own experience than the collective myth of a spiritual super-man who 'got it all right' in one blinding moment of *satori*. In fact it is more liberating for us as a religious society to know that in spite of incredible insight and clarity, he got some of it wrong and was guilty of neurotic overreaction in his attitude to 'hireling priests' (along with many of his contemporaries) and blind to the real significance of religious symbolism. It frees us to move out of insularity, unlearn inherited distrust and share in what the Holy Spirit is doing in other religious groups.

We do not know who or what the Hebrew poet had in mind when he wrote so profoundly of a quite different kind of healing, and saw, as Jürgen Moltmann has suggested, that 'basically, wounds are only healed by wounds'.[3] Whether it was a poignant tribute to some Hebrew martyr or part of his own struggle to find meaning in the broken and humiliated state of his own race we do not really know. His insight may have sprung from the ancient myth of the wounded healer, the keeper of the secret of wholeness, whose own wound remains mysteriously unhealed. All that we do know is that the Christian church was quick to recognise the features of the suffering servant of God in the one who had shown them the real cost of being human in a broken world. There is nothing strange about any of this. We live in a society which is still playing the same vicious game with those whose truth and integrity threaten the status quo.

In our own fragmented society the real healing of humanity takes place in the same costly way. The successful, the powerful and the righteous still oppress us and we only discover the seed of our own wholeness in the wasteland of self-doubt and isolation, when we wrestle with our own need to heal the world without the inconvenience of personal anguish. As Henri Nouwen has reminded us, 'the great illusion of leadership is to think that man can be led out of the desert by someone who has never been there'.[4]

The wilderness experience is part of the human journey, the place where we wrestle for the truths which enable us to heal our broken humanity and care for its victims, including ourselves. It is also the place in which angels minister to us, not the shining ones of Sunday-school illustrations with composed faces and not a wing out of place, but the human messengers of God who bring us telegrams of hope. Anyone who brings us life and healing is part of this angelic company whether it be a small child, a comedian or a fellow sufferer.

Edward Milligan, who has been one of my mentors in the past few years, teaching me so much about ministry and pastoral care and delivering a good many telegrams, puts it more gracefully than I can manage:

> Isolation of spirit . . . comes to most—perhaps all of us—at one time or another. There are times when the tides of faith seem far out, times of dryness, times when we do not feel the comfort and guidance of God's hand . . . I can think with thankfulness of Friends who brought light to my darkness—perhaps a single sentence, a friendly letter, a walk on the downs; their help was perhaps given unconsciously but it was because they were sensitive to God's leadings that they were able to do it. Do we seek to be channels of God's caring? Caring matters most.[5]

Von Hügel and Edward Milligan are right in reminding us that Christianity is about caring and that caring matters most. But we can easily forget that the word 'care' has its roots in the Gothic 'karôn', which means 'to lament'. Henri Nouwen points out that the basic meaning of 'care' is 'to grieve, to experience sorrow, to cry out with' and goes on to say that in western society we have associated caring with '. . . an attitude of the strong towards the weak, of the powerful towards the powerless, of the haves towards the have nots'.[6] It has not often been associated with the ability to deal honestly with our own fear of emotion and learn how to be vulnerable and open to the pain of others. We are often ill at ease in a situation which offers us an invitation to enter into another person's pain without having any answers and without *doing* something about it. We are fearful in case the encounter with violent human emotions re-opens old wounds and activates painful feelings which might overwhelm us. Yet the violence which is erupting in our own society is one symptom of the pain and frustration of a world situation which gives us reason enough for some of the acute feelings that are being unleashed. Our caring must be tough and tender enough to bear the torrent of anguish that is shaking us all.

Perhaps it is because we are more at ease dispensing the less searing brands of care that we have fallen into what Lionel Blue describes as the danger of romantic religion:

> It is traditionally more at home with a rural scene, the simple life and classic forms of charity and service—saintly men who offer cloaks to beggars. It has difficulty in turning away from the classical problems of poverty and persecution to the modern problems of leisure and affluence . . . As a result religious groups play safe. They scavenge the world for problems which admit of classical solutions. They have much to say about the third world, which is conveniently far, but little about the society to which they minister.[7]

Caring and ministry in a society as alienated from the sources of hope and real community as our own will not be effective unless we can risk the exposure of our own vulnerability and allow ourselves to be known as the incomplete and wounded human beings that we are. My own list of angels is one which includes many who have had that kind of courage—Elizabeth Kübler Ross, Harry Williams, Thomas Merton, Edwin Muir, as well as some I have discovered among the world family of Friends. They have encouraged and healed me by not being too afraid to show me their own broken humanity, the wounds of personal loss and failure, the scars of their neuroses, their painful wrestlings for reality. Confronted with the traumas of a planet in peril they have known that the real answer was not to be found in pious platitudes about the way things ought to be, even statements issued to the press and letters delivered personally to 10 Downing Street. Those who wrestle with God may well make statements later about the meaning of their struggles, but the thing one notices about them is that they limp rather badly but generally seem to know who they are. I have always had a soft spot for Jacob, wounds, warts and all, but chiefly because he reminds us that to be fully human involves being in touch with our pain, aware of our hang-ups and not afraid to face the dark side of ourselves.

I am not suggesting that it is always inappropriate to set truth as we see it in words that may challenge the values and assumptions of the powerful. That remains the prophetic role of every church, and never more so than in our own dehumanised society. I am suggesting that statements alone are not enough unless they issue from the kind of wrestling that involves us in change, in painful growth and the refusal to take any short cuts which dodge the uncomfortable and central symbol of our faith.

A paraplegic friend of mine once wrote:

> I believe that being made whole involves learning to absorb suffering instead of passing it on in another form . . . Suffering comes to us in the form of pain, frustration, ill-health and unhappiness, and we take part in the vicious circle of never-ending suffering by passing it on to other people in the forms of irritability, resentment, bitterness or cynicism. But hope for mankind will only come when we cease to do this, when we absorb the suffering that comes our way and render it powerless by refusing to pass it on to other people in some way. [8]

She was saying something crucial about the mystery that lies at the heart of the Christian story, and yet Christian stoicism is not enough for me, perhaps because I have never been able to manage it. I find more strong comfort in a community like the Society of Friends, in which the hurts and bruises which we give to one another (simply because we are unfinished creations, still struggling to grow and become more real) are accepted and healed by that tremendous tolerance for which we are known, and in the discipline we accept to struggle for truth and humorously accept our idiosyncratic and sometimes slightly dotty interpretations of it. I am even more comforted by the fact that there are Friends, who like Bonhoeffer, are willing to let me see the painful gap between their public and private selves.

What I do find missing in some of the meetings I visit is the other side of the passion story. Friends have a splendid reputation for their mediation work in international crisis situations and in the relief of suffering. It is rather less splendid when it comes to the business of celebration and festivity. Is this because we can cope well enough with the classical crisis situations in which it is clear what needs to be done, but are less able to cope with the more ambiguous human encounters in which there is nothing to be done at all except to listen and suffer with another person?

I have noticed that those who are most in touch with their own feelings, whether of grief or anger, who have worked through the pain without trying to dodge it or escape into chronic overwork, are also those who have passion for life—a zest for living that is not quenched by the tensions of living in a broken world. They have, I think, sensed a unity behind its brokenness which enables them to keep things in perspective. They have a relish for all that is good and wholesome, beautiful and comic in the human situation, and because they are human nothing is alien to them and nothing lost beyond the hope of retrieval. They may in fact say very little about God, yet they love the world in an inclusive way which seems to be a reflection of the way in which God loves it, distributing blessing without discrimination and caring most passionately for those who cannot believe themselves worth such consideration.

The *opposite* of real pain bearing and sharing, which as Paul reminds us is the way we actually fulfil the law of Christ,[9] is not joy and festivity but apathy, which is a symptom of disease. Jürgen Moltmann describes it as a characteristic sign of the sickness of western society and of many individuals in it and lists some of the results of it in those individuals. 'Interest in life is crippled . . . The "courage to be" is weakened. One withdraws into a cell, boxes oneself in, locks oneself up in order not to be exposed to suffering.'[10] He goes on to suggest that by far the most successful way of walling ourselves off from life is through non-stop activity, overwork and accomplishment. This is a form of self-sacrifice which is easily mistaken for the real renunciations of love, and it is one which receives the full approval of a society infected by the Protestant work ethic and our contemporary obsession with efficiency and success. It is also of course a society which is far less comfortable if we are human enough to 'weep with those who weep' or to sing in the high street when we are joyful.

When we become one-sided in our personal lives, unable to play or relax, we open ourselves to the dangers of insensitivity and depression. We are actually too tired to notice another person's difficulties or needs. 'We become incapable of love and incapable of sorrow.'[11] We are simply locked up in the prison of our own self-importance and extreme busyness, our crowded diaries and sheer exhaustion preventing us from celebrating the miracle of life and savouring it with real relish.

I have come to think that far from demonstrating our trust in God this kind of non-stop activity is often the work of those twin demons of guilt and arrogance. Friends are peculiarly prone to the kind of guilt which makes them uneasy about enjoying themselves or saying 'no' to requests for help. Nor are we immune to the arrogance which imagines that the world will collapse without our continual interference in its affairs or that God is unable to cope without our non-stop support and activity.

At a recent QHS Representative Council one member shared the story of a Friend in her local meeting who felt weighed down with commitments, exhausted by taking on more and more work on behalf of Quaker committees or answering appeals for help from various quarters. In some despair she went for a walk and wrestled with God about this. In the end she heard herself addressed by name and an amused and compassionate voice within her said: '*How* do you think I managed before you were born?'

It is difficult to keep a sense of proportion and laugh at our absurdities when we are so acutely aware of the conflict and pain in our world. Our ministry and caring are needed and yet in attempting to do more than God's will for us we shall be in danger of losing our peace and merely adding to the world's confusion:

> There is, it sometimes seems, an excess of busyness these days, a round of committees and conferences and journeyings of which the cost in peaceable wisdom is not sufficiently counted. Sometimes we appear overmuch to count as merit our participation in these things . . . True leisureliness is a beautiful thing and may not lightly be given away. Indeed it is one of the outstanding and most wonderful features in the life of Christ that with all his work in healing and preaching and planning for the kingdom he leaves behind a sense of leisure, of time in which to pray and meditate, to stand and stare at the cornfields and fishing boats and listen to the confidences of neighbours and passers by. [12]

When I first read the Gospels as a teenager unconditioned by long association with the church I can recall a similar astonishment that this person whom Christians called Lord or Saviour of humanity was, as far as I could see, very different from the rather mirthless Christianity I had glimpsed in evangelical rallies and Sunday-schools. I was amazed to find a man who took time off from pastoral care in order to birdwatch and marvel at flowers, to go to parties and watch small children at play. It was not my image of a conventional holy man any more than it was for his first friends and critics.

I was equally amazed at the number of occasions when he said that the Kingdom of God was like a rather large party and described his own ministry as festival in which gloom and fasting were as out of place as they would be at a wedding feast. It came as a shock of surprise from which I have never properly recovered.

There was no shortage of international conflict or social injustice in the world in which he lived nor any shortage of compassion in his encounters with those who were the victims of it. His ability to enter into the pain of others and bring wholeness was surely the other side of a passion for life which claimed no immunity from any part of it and celebrated each with the same wholeheartedness, even to the extent of allowing himself to be broken by others. But, as Lionel Blue reminded his listeners in a recent broadcast, after that event his first ministry to his grieving friends is to invite them to celebrate the miracle of new life with 'a fish barbecue on the beach'.

NOTES

1   *The Wounded Healer* (New York: Doubleday and Co, 1972), cited Howard Clinebell, *Growth Counselling* (Nashville: Abingdon, 1979), p. 71.
2   *Good News Bible* (Collins, 1976).
3   *The Open Church: Invitation to a Messianic Life Style* (London: SCM, 1978), p. 25.
4   *The Wounded Healer*, p. 73.
5   Edward H. Milligan, in *Christian Faith and Practice in the Experience of the Society of Friends* (London Yearly Meeting, 1960), §340.
6   Henri Nouwen, *Out of Solitude* (Indiana: Ave Maria/Notre Dame, 1974), p. 34.
7   Lionel Blue, *To Heaven with the Scribes and Pharisees* (London: Darton, Longman and Todd, 1975), p. 11.
8   Audrey Shepherd, *Stigma—The Experience of Disability*, ed. Paul Hunt (London: Geoffrey Chapman, 1966), p. 66.
9   Galatians 6, 2, Revised Standard Version.
10 *The Open Church* . . ., p. 20.
11 *The Open Church* . . . . p. 21.
12 Caroline C.Graveson, in *Christian Faith and Practice in the Experience of the Society of Friends* (London Yearly Meeting, 1960), §§458.

RATHER ODD PEOPLE

by Elfrida Vipont Foulds

One of the interesting things about being an octogenarian and a Quaker is that you suddenly find that some of your perfectly ordinary memories have turned into Quaker history. Another is that you suddenly find the answers to questions that have been puzzling you for the last seventy or eighty years. Like the little incident with Miss Thompson in the kindergarten, for instance, which has been nagging away at my conscience ever since the early nineteen hundreds. I can still see my little classmate's hand shooting up: 'What's a Quaker, Miss Thompson?' she asked. Miss Thompson hesitated. 'Oh–er–they're rather odd people, aren't they, Elfrida?' she said. The other children looked at me curiously. What was I supposed to say? Was I odd? Were my parents, my brothers and cousins odd? How was I to know? It would be safer to make the routine answer to the all-knowing grown-up. 'Yes, Miss Thompson,' I said.

The dilemma long rankled in my infant Quaker conscience. What ought I to have said? It has taken me nearly four-score years to find out. I knew about Quakers, of course. Every Sunday morning my brothers and I mounted to the top deck of an electric tram-car with our mother to attend meeting at Mount Street in Manchester. Our father was always a little late because he first had to attend the Adult School in West Gorton.* I grew up with an intense dislike of the Adult School movement because it was responsible for my father's absence first thing on Sunday morning. Every other day of the week he was out of the house first thing in the morning because of his medical practice, so this should have been his only unhurried breakfast. The Adult School was also responsible for my mother's frequent absences on Sunday afternoon, when she very often conducted

*Elfrida Vipont Foulds's parents were
Edward Vipont Brown (1863-1955) and
Dorothy Brown, née Crowley (1874-1968).

the women's class. It never struck me as strange that men's classes and women's classes should be held separately, because that was the way things were. In Mount Street the two sides of the meeting house were called the men's side and the women's side, and there was a men's lobby and a women's lobby. I cannot actually remember the men and women sitting separately in meeting, because long before I was born my parents led a rebellion which resulted in husbands and wives crossing the gangway one way or the other and sitting defiantly together. 'We sat on the women's side and the Grahams sat on the men's side,' said my mother, and apparently that was that, though an element of separation survived when I was a child. The lobbies were still sacrosanct, but presumably this was occasioned by the position of the men's and women's cloakrooms.

Where you sat in meeting was important in those days. All the long white beards sat facing the meeting on one side, and all the beady bonnets and mantles on the other. They always sat in the same seats, and opposite them all the families sat invariably in the same rows. When I was a little older I would attend meeting in an agony of apprehension if I happened to find myself at the head of the family procession. 'Fifth row from the front,' I would mumble to myself. 'One–two–three–four–five–oh, did Mother say five or was it six?' I would hesitate, panic-stricken, and then a comforting shove would propel me into the right row, next to the end, and, 'Leave a place for Daddy,' whispered my mother.

The row of beards tended to be rather terrifying, though there was one wonderful old Friend called Charles Garnett, with a long snow-white beard, who always brought a pocketful of sweets to give to the children after meeting. Another long but rather wispy beard belonged to a Friend I always called Father Christmas, though his name was Walker Unsworth. He cannot have been quite as aged as he looked, for I remember John Robson telling me that eventually he migrated into Yorkshire where John as a Young Friend, glorying in his first motor-cycle, offered him a lift home from meeting in the old-fashioned, wicker-covered side-car, only to be greeted by every small boy in sight with, 'Sithee—look—theer's Moses in t'basket!' Another elderly Friend used to terrify me by exclaiming as soon as he caught sight of me, 'Thou art in the pedigree!' I had no idea what a pedigree was, it might have been the Rogue's Gallery so far as I was concerned, but I did at least fare better than my friends Rachel and Agnes Graham, to whom he would announce loudly, 'Agnes the lamb, and Rachel the ewe lamb.' Which infuriated Rachel almost beyond bearing. This Friend was Joseph Spence Hodgson, a distant cousin of my father's with a passion for tracing family connections. In 1898, at the opening of the new swimming bath at Ackworth, to the astonishment of the assembled company he had interrupted his speech by plunging in wearing a top-hat and a frock coat. He appears in old photographs surrounded by cats, but unfortunately, he did not bring his cats to meeting.

The importance of sitting in the right place gradually died out in Mount Street meeting house, which was just as well, for my mother used to assure me that when she first came to Mount Street meeting, new Friends were warned not to sit in seats formerly occupied by deceased Friends, and if this rule had persisted there might have been no room for the living. It must, however, have persisted longer in more remote places if my father's experience is anything to go by. I may as well give the correct source of this story, which has been told of many well-known Friends. I am qualified to do so as I was at home when he returned, still chuckling, having entered a large meeting house in the south-west of England to attend meeting for worship. Finding not a soul there, he settled down quietly to hold a meeting by himself. After some considerable time he heard the door open, followed by the sound of soft, shuffling footsteps. After a while, a hand touched his shoulder and he looked up to see an aged couple standing by his side, obviously in great perplexity. 'Excuse me, Friend,' said the old man at last, 'thou art sitting in my place!'

Even at Mount Street, the beards and beady bonnets did not always give way when the younger Friends suggested changes. Remembering my father's customary late arrival at meeting for worship—even he needed a little time to cycle from West Gorton to Mount Street, and other Friends were similarly circumstanced—I once asked my mother why Mount Street Friends had never thought of changing the time of meeting for worship.

'Oh, but we did!' she exclaimed, following her remark with the little chuckle which indicated that she 'could a tale unfold'.

'Then why didn't they do it?' I enquired.

'We asked for meeting to be at eleven o'clock,' she said. 'We said that lots of meetings started at eleven.'

'Then what happened?' I asked.

'Oh, they agreed,' she said. 'But after a few weeks the old women Friends complained of the waste of time involved, because of course they were all dressed for meeting at the usual time and then they had to sit in their drawing-rooms in their bonnets and mantles and *wait* for half an hour. And the old men Friends waited too, with their top hats at the ready. It was all very sad—but we had to go back to the old time.'

None of these things seemed strange to me when I was young. I just took it for granted that my elders and betters behaved like that, just as I took it for granted that the older members of the meeting would almost invariably address me in the 'plain tongue'. The Graham family, including the children, seldom used anything else. I remember how puzzled I was when I overheard a lady say to my mother, 'What *do* you think I heard the other day? Such a funny thing! Those little Graham girls were setting off for school and Rachel was shouting, "Oh Agnes, *wilt* thou buck up?"' Now what on earth was funny about *that*, I wondered.

John William Graham and my father were firm friends, and they both belonged to the group of Friends who supported John Wilhelm Rowntree in the great re-awakening of Quakerism at the turn of the century. I doubt if I fully realised the tremendous force of the movement on the Friends who experienced it until I heard my father, in his extreme old age, exclaim on hearing me refer to John Wilhelm Rowntree's early death: 'He was our *leader*!' It made me understand that John Wilhelm Rowntree was no spent force in the hearts of those who had known him.

The summer schools which followed the Manchester Conference also involved my parents and led to my father's life-long enthusiasm for Bible study. It was not until I came across a journal kept by my mother during the years before I was born that I realised how the young people who attended these gatherings enjoyed not only inspiration but a good deal of fun into the bargain. They took their bicycles with them as well as their Bibles and spent the afternoons in hilarious excursions along the dusty roads outside Scarborough or Birmingham. For many of them, including my father, to attend a summer school involved sacrificing most of their annual summer holiday, which was brief enough in any case. The same sacrifice was involved for those attending Yearly Meeting, which probably explains why, as fewer Friends were self-employed, Yearly Meetings began to get shorter and more business-like.

My father used to tell me how, in 1893, he had attended Yearly Meeting because he knew John William Graham could not be there, and they both felt very strongly a concern that London Yearly Meeting should recognise the Hicksite Friends in America. John William Graham had visited the United States and enjoyed opportunities for travel amongst the Hicksite Friends, with whom he had found spiritual fellowship. The path for reconciliation seemed clear, and my father, full of enthusiasm, promised to attend Yearly Meeting and share the concern with the gathering. He was not allowed to get very far. The idea of such a reconciliation so shocked the assembled Friends that he was silenced by the Clerk, an experience that rankled in the young man's heart for many years.

John William Graham was not only ahead of his time in his Quaker witness. Some of his ideas seemed very strange to his contemporaries, and even his fellow members of the meeting and the students at Dalton Hall, where he was Principal, made fun of them. For instance, he was convinced that industrial smoke was injurious to health and that smoke abatement was essential for the building up of a healthy population. Such an idea was hardly likely to be popular in a manufacturing community! Even odder in the eyes of many of his friends was his support, some years before it became generally accepted, for the idea of daylight saving. His enthusiasm was such that he organised his family life during the holidays on daylight-saving lines. We all thought this was very funny, and were sure that the Grahams would never keep it up, but they did. And, of course, by 1916 everybody had to follow suit.

When what we used to call the Great War broke out in 1914, most people said it would be over by Christmas. My parents were not so sure. Manchester Friends campaigned vigorously to prevent war from starting, and then campaigned with equal vigour to bring it to an end. I found myself in a dilemma. I was barely twelve years old at the time, and over the years I had collected what I considered to be a formidable array of toy soldiers. My parents were by no means in favour of such toys. Indeed, my father had taken care to discourage my elder brothers from playing with soldiers, but it did not occur to him that he would need to warn his daughter against it—little girls played with dolls. This little girl didn't. I bought soldiers at a penny each, one by one, with my pocket money: I mended them with matchsticks when their heads came off; I took them for perilous voyages across the linoleum in an old shoe-box; their adventures were part of my life.

'What about thy soldiers now?' asked my mother curiously.

Something had to be done about such a situation by an infant pacifist.

'They're not soldiers any more,' I said. 'They're Members of Parliament.'

As I look back on the activities of Manchester Friends during the First World War, I often wonder if they could have sustained them, or even attempted them, without the impetus of the Manchester Conference and the subsequent re-awakening of Quakerism behind them. I remember innumerable Peace Meetings to which gradually more and more people came, some held in Mount Street meeting house and some in the open air. The only place where the citizens of Manchester could hold open-air meetings without police permission was Stevenson Square, and the Friends joined with the Women's International League and other peace-loving bodies in holding peace meetings addressed by dauntless speakers standing on lorries. Sometimes the meetings were attacked and scattered by 'rowdies', which was very exciting and I was disappointed when I was absent on these occasions, as I generally was because of school. Manchester Friends were always on the lookout for jobs which nobody else would do, and I remember being taken on several occasions to visit a convalescent home for Belgian soldiers which was run temporarily and very efficiently by women Friends because nobody else would undertake it. The situation must have bristled with difficulties, but Manchester

Friends did not seem to be aware of them. During the first Christmas of the war, Manchester Friends held a party at Mount Street meeting house for the wives and children of interned Germans. It was a huge success. Father Christmas appeared, resplendent in my father's scarlet academic robes, the German children sang well and the Quaker children sang badly, and a good time was had by all. Next year it was not possible to collect so many 'enemy aliens' in one place, and parcels were distributed instead.

The situation rapidly worsened. Friends meetings may not always have been completely united in their witness for peace, but they were united in their love for one another. The Peace Meetings continued, and Mount Street meeting house, the one place where peace workers of every religious sect or none could be sure of a platform, had the distinction of being mobbed. Friends attending London committees brought back stirring tales of the situation there. My favourite hero at the time was Baroness Orczy's Scarlet Pimpernel, but when I learnt of a Manchester Friend well known to me, Constance Crosland, conveying confidential documents in and out of Devonshire House (the historic precursor of Friends House) concealed in her substantial underwear, I realised that there were more types than one of heroes and heroines. When on one occasion I accompanied my mother to London, where she was attending Meeting for Sufferings, I was not asked to carry documents in my equally substantial school knickers, but I did experience an air raid by planes with what were then called torpedoes. As I had already experienced air raids by zeppelins, which were very noisy affairs, I made nothing of it and my mother and I stayed in bed, but a Friend called Shipley Brayshaw, who was staying in the same hotel, told us next day that a number of Friends and other visitors had sought refuge in the basement—'some of them,' he added in shocked tones, 'in *night attire*!'.

Shipley Brayshaw was a Friend with a quite unusual depth of human understanding. I remember a monthly meeting I attended after the war when elders reported the receipt of an astonishingly rude letter from a Young Friend who announced that he was resigning his membership and going off to join the Red (Russian) Army. Friends were deeply shocked by this truculent missive. They could think of no possible response to make except to record acceptance of the letter. At last Shipley Brayshaw rose to his feet. 'Yes,' he said in his familiar sing-song voice, 'we must record the resignation, but we must be careful to *leave the door open*. Perhaps when he gets there, our Young Friend may not *like* the Red Army, in which case it will be important for him to know that we shall welcome him back.' He didn't like the Red Army, and eventually we duly welcomed him back.

At the end of the war I had still not attained the status of a 'Young Friend'. You did not qualify for this until you had left school, and once having attained it you held on to it until you were married or middle-aged. Nevertheless, I was proud to be involved in some of the developments which proved that the influence of the Manchester Conference was still vibrant and that new developments were on the way. I remember attending two Easter conferences with my parents when I was still a schoolgirl. They were arranged by the Yorkshire 1905 Committee, the precursor of the Yorkshire Friends Service Committee, and one was held at Skipton and the other at Bentham. I remember the one at Skipton was attended by a number of conscientious objectors fresh from prison; it was also attended by a Friend I had never heard of before, called Carl Heath. It was there, at Skipton, that Carl Heath produced his idea for 'Quaker Embassies' which fired the imagination of a whole generation of Young Friends and led to the development of Quaker centres in various parts of the world.

Immediately after I left school came the first World Conference of Friends, then called the All-Friends Conference. Though nothing like so representative as those which were to follow, it brought Friends together in an unprecedented way. I was not eligible to attend it, but I went to the Young Friends Conference at Jordans, which was held at the same time and was visited by some of the same speakers. I remember rushing out and climbing a tree to get a sight of the first German Young Friends I had ever encountered.

Quaker centres—world conferences—this was a whole new phase in the existence of the Society of Friends, one in which I was to grow up and find a place and such service as I could render. A new phase it was indeed, but it could not have developed without the influence of that earlier generation of Friends who broke into history with the Manchester Conference.

But what has all this to do with Miss Thompson's, 'They're rather odd people, aren't they, Elfrida?' and my secret shame at having evaded it? The right answer to Miss Thompson has always been there, of course, but one does not learn it by rote, and one does not inherit it; it has to be lived in, and that takes time. From George Fox's, 'Christ saith this and the apostles say this, but what canst thou say?' to the Advices and Queries' 'Do not let the fear of seeming peculiar influence your decision,' Quakers have endeavoured to live out their witness in great issues and in small, in season and out of season, against all probability and sometimes against all common sense. Yes, Miss Thompson, Quakers are odd people, gloriously and unashamedly odd.

QUAKERS IN THE LOOKING-GLASS OF THE STAGE

by Ormerod Greenwood

The stage Quaker shares with the stage Irishman and the stage parson a perennial quality, rejected of course by real Quakers, Irishmen and the clergy, yet by its persistence suggesting that the stage Obadiahs, Teagues and Canon Chasubles have some element of truth in caricature which validates them or endears them to their public. The very fact of creating a stereotype confers a kind of immortality—the personage need not even appear on the stage but merely be referred to, like Mrs Grundy in Thomas Morton's *Speed the Plough* (1800): 'What will Mrs Grundy zay? What will Mrs Grundy think?' (Act I, Sc. 1). The Quaker equivalent—though he does appear in the last act of the play—is the real Simon Pure, from Pennsylvania, in Susannah Centlivre's *A Bold Stroke for a Wife* (1718): 'I do affirm that I am Simon Pure', says the imposter. 'Thy name may be Pure, friend, but not that Pure', declares the real Simon. This play also provides the original Quaker 'Obadiah' in Obadiah Prim, one of the four guardians whose consent must be won before Colonel Farnwell can marry the lovely Ann Lovely.

Of course it was inconceivable, since every Friend from George Fox and Robert Barclay had set their faces against the iniquity of stage plays, that a play about Quakers, or in which they were represented, would ever be written by a Quaker or even an attender, down to the twentieth century. (The present writer was warned against the moral dangers of the stage as late as 1930.) The only inside knowledge could come from a renegade or one brought up among Friends, the only observation from personal friendship or casual acquaintance or business relationship. No one in the late seventeenth century, the eighteenth or nineteenth centuries, ever tried to describe from the inside what it is like to be a Quaker; what moral or ethical dilemmas it poses to be one; what shapes our common humanity to the Quaker frame; or what the life of so small and intimate a group produces in the way of social pressures. Finding out what Quakers were really like was not the object of the playwrights or their audience. They were content with curiosity, with the fun that could be got out of the peculiar dress, language and manners of the Quakers, with satire at the expense of their claims to be above and beyond human weakness, never to swear and always to speak the truth. There is mockery of their hope to be led by the Spirit; delight in demonstrating that in lechery, meanness, cunning and hypocrisy they are not only no better, but sometimes considerably worse, than their fellow human beings; pleasure in contrasting their assumed gravity with situations that provoke levity. Quaker speech, habits and dress meant that they were easily picked out for ridicule or for mimicry, or to lend local colour to a stock situation. Dramatists soon discovered their value for purposes of plotting. To have someone (lady or gent.) disguised as a Quaker; or for a change to have a Quaker (lady or gent.) disguised as *not* a Quaker; these stratagems solved with a degree of verisimilitude many a knotty turn in the story. The Quaker who does not swear, and the parrot who does, became a recurrent stage joke, like Wigan pier or mother-in-law in the later repertoire of the music-hall. Both the disguise and the parrot are used by Susannah Centlivre in *The Beau's Duel* (1702) where Mrs Plotwell, disguised as a Quakeress, converts a parrot:

> TOBER: . . . yesterday I carried her to wait on a relation of ours that has a parrot, and whilst I was discoursing about some private business, she converted the bird and now it talks of nothing but the Light of the Spirit and the Inward Man. Ha, ha!

Comical opportunities abound also in the situations of characters obliged to adopt Quaker disguise, and therefore called on at short notice (or none at all) to become adepts in using the plain language and adopting Quaker piety. Such is the situation of the unfortunate Sir Feeble Goodwill while courting the rich Quakeress, Widow Purelite, in Richard Williamson's *Vice Reclaim'd; or, The Passionate Mistress* (1703)—but at least they are rewarded with a dance of five Quakers at the wedding. Gamont in Mary Davy's *The Northern Heiress; or, The Humours of York* (1716) complains of his lot:

> How the Devil came I to stumble upon so much morality today! Gravity is not my talent . . . I shall have nothing else to keep me from hanging myself, unless I turn speaker at a Quaker meeting, and renounce the flesh for the spirit.

76

The fun sometimes becomes scurrilous, as in Charles Knipe's *A City Ramble; or, The Humours of the Compter* (1715) with drunkenness and adultery as the background. In this play, as in some others, the female of the species gets as hard knocks as the male, but there is a notable tendency almost from the start for Quakeresses to be treated rather more gently, as they look shyly out from their bonnets on the wicked world, and occasionally use their simplicity to get the better of their wily enemies—not so green as they seem, which is always a rewarding dramatic theme. The tendency is evident in Charles Shadwell's title, *The Fair Quaker of Deal; or, The Humours of the Navy* (1710) though Dorcas ends, in fact, by marrying a churchman. The later eighteenth century, with its cults of sentimentality and philanthropy, turns soft on the Quakers and begins to smile on them as well as smiling at them—even looks at actual Quakers and makes portraits of them. Thus Samuel Foote, whose fierce caricatures roused Dr Johnson's wrath, larded his play against doctors, which continues the tradition stretching from Molière to Bernard Shaw, with a character called Dr Melchisedek Broadbrim based on John Fordyce, Quaker member of a famous medical family of the time. The play is called *The Devil on Two Sticks* (1768) but the title has only a punning allusion to the better-known work of Le Sage which bears the same name. John O'Keeffe may have modelled his rakish Quaker hero, Young Sadboy in *The Young Quaker* (1783)—plain in speech but deplorable in behaviour—on one of those Penn lads who gave us such a bad name (the brothers Thomas and William Penn III). But the heroine, the young Quakeress Dinah Primrose, is a good girl even though Old Sadboy in America did not approve of her, and in fact sent his son to London to break off relations with her; if the father had possessed even a modicum of traditional Quaker sagacity he might have known *that* would not work. The play ends with a rousing anti-slavery speech, plain evidence that we are into a different era. John O'Keeffe's other Quaker heroine, in *Wild Oats* (1791), became familiar to modern audiences through the 1977 revival by the Royal Shakespeare Company, with Lisa Harrow playing the charmingly demure 'devout Quakeress', Lady Amaranth, abounding in wealth and piety; and Alan Howard the strolling Rover, with a quotation from the repertoire for every situation.

Another popular playwright who looks benevolently on Friends is the elder Charles Dibdin (1748-1814)—an irascible and quarrelsome man, but composer of some of the sweetest and most touching popular songs in the language, many inspired by his seafaring brother Tom who died on a voyage home from the Cape, struck by lightning: *Tom Bowling; Blow High, Blow Low*; *Poor Jack*. Dibdin's heroine in *The Quaker* (1777) is Gillian, who is in the predicament familiar to young women of the time in life and in story: she is promised by her father to the elderly Friend Steady, but loves young Lubin. Steady, however, turns up trumps as an elderly Quaker *should* (and in life often *does*). He secretly helps the young lovers, and outwits the traps set for them, and we are treated to a May party on a Quaker's lawn for a bonus. Dibdin still manages to get plenty of comic relief out of our peculiarities.

The highest Romantic tribute to Quaker benevolence comes from abroad, in Alfred de Vigny's *Chatterton* (1834)—perhaps the greatest success of the Paris theatre at the time, though like other French plays it has found difficult the passage of the Channel. The play is based, very loosely, on the suicide of the English poet Thomas Chatterton, 'forger' (or creator, if you like) of the Rowley poems. He is a lodger in the London house of the prosperous, middle-aged entrepreneur, John Bell. Bell's wife, Kitty, is in the predicament that awaited Charles Dibdin's Gillian: she is married to a man thirty years older than herself, and terrified of him. Inevitably she is attracted by the mysterious, sick, sad, starving young poet upstairs, and there is an unspoken, un-physical, impalpable love affair between them which ends in the death of both. A narrator and commentator and intermediary in the action is 'The Quaker' (never named) whose presence in the house is explained by the fact that he saved the Bells' son from death by his skill as a doctor, and has given away his wealth in the same spirit as John Woolman and Daniel Wheeler. The Quaker, perhaps too perfect an embodiment of wisdom and patience, but saved by a little asperity, embodies the concept of the idealised Quaker derived from Voltaire's *Letters on the English Nation*. Alfred de Vigny, who had lived in England and married an English (or more exactly, Creole) wife, had opportunities of observing us at first hand. His wonderful twenty-two-year-old heroine, Kitty, was created with complete success by his thirty-seven-year-old mistress, Marie Dorval, making the imaginative leap into the skin of an evangelical background of spotless purity and unworldly timidity.

With the next playwright, James Sheridan Knowles (1784-1862), we are over the hill of High Romanticism, and into the plain of the Victorian age. Knowles was Irish, born in Cork, his father was a cousin of R.B.Sheridan; he knew the extremes of success and failure like so many theatre people, was by turns doctor, actor, teacher, playwright, and in the end Baptist preacher. There is an unforgettable portrait of him in old age in Edmund Gosse's *Father and Son*. Most of his plays are tragedies, many written for that eminent Victorian actor Macready; but his Quaker play, *Woman's Wit* (1838), is a comedy. Its plot is melodramatic, its blank verse mostly fustian, but its Quaker scenes are very, very funny and it would be good to see it revived in the spirit of *Wild Oats*. Here we have the double disguise: a real Quaker, Helen Mowbray, disguised as a boy, Eustace, and learning fencing to get her own back on the wicked Lord Athunree, who has blackened her name; whilst her friend, Hero Sutton, for her own reasons, disguises herself as a Quaker, which she is not. Helen's fencing is inadequate as you might expect; and at the fencing school she and another pupil, Walsingham, fall in love, with all those awkward homosexual overtones which Shakespeare alone knew how to manage. Walsingham's fencing, too, might have been inadequate against the masterly Lord Athunree in the duel, but Hero's uncle, Sir William Sutton, has got wind of it and sends the officers just in time. Hero, like her Quaker friend, has also been susceptible to the caddish charm of the Lord, and dances with him at the ball in sensuous abandonment, thereby imperilling the love of the 'good' suitor, Valentine. To get him back, she adopts the Quaker disguise with the help of her clever servant, Mr Clever, who makes a convincingly impressive elder. What fun they have, to be sure! Ruth Mapleson is Hero's Quaker name, and in the end Walsingham wins both Quakeress and high-born elegant lady even though he goes back on his promise to prefer the former.

We have reached the eighteen-nineties, for each period, as it seems, has its Quaker plays. Henry Arthur Jones, once famous from his melodrama *The Silver King* ('call back yesterday'), was a friend of Bernard Shaw and a benefactor to the theatre; he has been called 'the real initiator of the revival of dramatic art in England'. The Celtic influence persists, for his family (as his name shows) came from Wales, though he was born in Buckinghamshire. His Quaker play, *The Dancing Girl* (1891), was a great success at the Haymarket with Tree in the leading role of the Duke of Guisebury, and ran for 310 nights, a very long run by nineties standards. An allusion in the play to Herbert Spencer led to acquaintance and friendship between the playwright and that once-famous philosopher.

George Bernard Shaw was closely contemporary with Henry Arthur Jones; his dates are 1856-1950, but for our purpose he is a twentieth-century playwright. He declared a regard for the Quakers, and said that if he had a religious profession it would be ours; and he seemed on the brink of writing a Quaker play in *Major Barbara* (1905) when he found the Salvation Army more dramatic, and in *Saint Joan* (1924) when he found the Middle Ages more colourful. It was not until 1939 that *In Good King Charles's Golden Days* introduced our founder, George Fox, to the stage along with other figures of the Restoration period. The play is really a sort of Platonic dialogue, and Shaw is too canny an old hand to try and reproduce period speech—but what is Fox without that speech as full of flavour as a Blenheim Orange pippin? He talks robust good sense in the play, as he generally did in life, but it is Shavian good sense, not his own, and the mysterious hinterland of the numinous, which in his life lay behind each phrase, is not there in Shaw.

A new and deeper note is struck in the last of our examples, the play *US* (1966), which was given at the Aldwych Theatre in London under the direction of Peter Brook, who described the play, a kind of drama-documentary on the Vietnam War, as 'a collaboration'. 'We have attempted together to understand a situation too vast to encompass alone, and too painful to ignore,' he wrote in a programme note. J.W.Lambert, reviewing the performance in *Drama* (Winter 1966, p. 20) said:

> The first half of *US* made its deepest mark not in its brisk tendentious scraps but in the re-creation (from the transcript of a tape) of a Quaker prayer-meeting held in the United States by the family and friends, and notably the widow, of a young American who, emulating the Oriental protest, had burnt himself to death. Here the dramatic temperature rose sharply, and with it our response to the humane issues involved. Now we could feel and share the pain, we were not merely being told facts, or told what to feel.

The young man who burnt himself to death on the steps of the Pentagon, having first put aside his own child, Emily—symbol of the Vietnamese children burnt by napalm—was Norman Morrison; and those of us who know his widow, Anne, are not surprised at the impact she made both in life and on the stage of the Aldwych Theatre. J.W.Lambert's review is a tribute to the Quaker method as well as to its dramatic power. The way is now open at last to a Quaker playwright to make creative as well as documentary use of the Quaker experience.

BIBLIOGRAPHICAL SUMMARY

These notes of Quaker plays, that is, plays in which Quakers *appear*, owe much to two pioneering articles:

W.W.Comfort, 'Some Stage Quakers'. Address to the Annual Meeting of the Friends Historical Association, 1924, printed in *Bulletin of FHA*, 24, no. 1 (Spring 1925).

Ezra Kempton Maxfield, 'The Quakers in English Stage Plays before 1800', *Publications of the Modern Language Association* (March 1930), pp. 256-73.

Additions to the following list would be welcomed. ('Musicals' have been omitted.)

There are many plays of the late seventeenth century in which Quakers are *mentioned* (Wycherley, *The Country Wife;* Vanbrugh, *The Provok'd Wife;* Congreve, *The Way of the World*, &c, &c, the last of these including the 'parrot' joke); but the first play to include Quaker characters is said to be:

John LEANORD

1. *The Country Innocence; or, The Chambermaid Turned Quaker* (1677).

This play is a revamping of Anthony Brewer's earlier play, *The Country Girl* (1647), which cannot have included Quakers. I have not seen this play, or several others in the list, but there is a copy in the library of Haverford College. According to Maxfield it reflects adversely on Quaker hypocrisy in the heroine, Mab, on the nasal tones of Quaker ministry, and on the cowardice of Mab's lover Rash, who 'turns the other cheek'.

Tom DURFEY (1653-1723)
2. *The Virtuous Wife; or, Good Luck at Last* (1680).
3. *The Richmond Heiress; or, A Woman Once in the Right* (1693).
4. *Two Queens of Brentford; or, Bayes No Poetaster.*
    A comic opera, published posthumously, and written presumably in the late 1670s as it is described as a reply to Buckingham's burlesque, *The Rehearsal* (1675).

Thomas SCOTT
5. *The Mock Marriage* (1696).

Richard WILLIAMSON
6. *Vice Reclaim'd; or, The Passionate Mistress* (1703).

Susannah CENTLIVRE (1667-1723)
7. *The Beau's Duel* (1702).
    Adapted from Jaspar Mayne's *The City Match* (1629), which cannot have contained Quakers.
8. *The Gotham Election* (1715), later called *The Humours of Elections.*
    Described by Allardyce Nicoll in his *History of Early Eighteenth-Century Drama* (1925) as 'of no value whatever'.
9. *A Bold Stroke for a Wife* (1718).
    After 'several gay adventures' Susannah, whose original maiden name is disputed, but who is said to have married first a Mr Carroll, found security in the arms of Queen Anne's cook, Joseph Centlivre. She is one of the most interesting of the many eighteenth-century lady dramatists. A 'droll' version of her masterpiece, *A Bold Stroke for a Wife*, is to be found in *The Stroller's Pacquet* (1741) under the title *The Guardians Over-reach'd in Their Own Humour; or, The Lover Metamorphosed*. (A 'droll' is a shortened, pirated version for country actors.)

Charles SHADWELL
10. *The Fair Quaker of Deal; or, The Humours of the Navy* (1710).
    A much-altered version by 'Captain Edward Thompson' dates from 1775 and has a new character suggested by Garrick, 'Dick Binnacle'.

Charles KNIPE
11. *The City Ramble; or, The Humours of the Compter* (1715).

Mary DAVYS
12. *The Northern Heiress; or, The Humours of York* (1716).

Samuel FOOTE (1720-77)
13. *The Devil upon Two Sticks* (1768).

John O'KEEFFE (1747-1833)
14. *Wild Oats; or, The Strolling Gentleman* (1771).
15. *The Young Quaker* (1783).

Charles DIBDIN (the elder) (1745-1814)
16. *The Quaker* (1777).

John MURDOCK (American playwright)
17. *The Triumphs of Love; or, The Happy Reconciler* (1795).

Alfred de VIGNY (1797-1863)
18. *Chatterton* (1834).

James Sheridan KNOWLES (1784-1862)
19. *Woman's Wit; or, Love's Disguises* (1838).

Harriet Beecher STOWE (1811-96)
20. *Uncle Tom's Cabin* (1852).
    Although this is properly a novel, it must be included because of the popularity of many stage versions, such as, for example, *Uncle Tom's Cabin; or, Life Among the*

Lowly by George L. Aiken. Simeon Halliday and his wife, Rachel, are based on the real-life family of Levi Coffin, styled 'President of the Underground Railroad'.

Henry Arthur JONES (1851-1929)
21. *The Dancing Girl* (1891).

George Bernard SHAW (1856-1950)
22. *In Good King Charles's Golden Days* (1939).

Peter BROOK and others
23. *US* (1966).

ENGLISH AND IRISH QUAKERS AND IRISH HOME RULE 1886-93

by Howard F.Gregg

Quakerism took root in Ireland in the aftermath of the Cromwellian conquest, its adherents being mostly English settlers or members of Cromwell's armies.[1] Thereafter Quakers established themselves, religiously and economically, within the Protestant community in Ireland. By keeping apart from both politics and religious tensions they were enabled to play a distinctive role in times of crisis, most notably during the 1798 Rebellion and the Great Famine of 1845-50.[2] Events in Ireland after 1869 broke this neutrality down. This essay will consider English and Irish Quaker responses to Gladstone's Home Rule Bills of 1886 and 1893.

For various reasons the Act of Union of 1800 failed to establish itself as the means for improved Anglo-Irish understanding or effective constitutional, social and economic relations.[3] The product of the aftermath of the 1798 Rebellion and Britain's strategic needs, the Act failed to satisfy the wishes of the Roman Catholic majority in Ireland for equal civil and political rights. It established the dominance of Britain as the senior partner and placed the interests of the Irish Protestant minority in dependence upon British support. By 1850 the Union had been seriously weakened by Roman Catholic Emancipation in 1829 and the Great Famine of 1845-50. From 1848 to 1916 it also faced the challenge of a revived Irish nationalism in both the constitutional and violent, separatist traditions. Home Rule was to prove the most serious constitutional challenge to the

Union between 1870 and 1912. Gladstone's decision of 1886 to support Irish Home Rule was the final blow in a series of shocks for the Irish Protestant minority.

O'Connell's success with the achievement of Emancipation in 1829 had begun the slow process by which the majority Catholic community gained political control in Ireland, outside Eastern Ulster.[4] The 1880 General Election saw the Protestant monopoly of Irish constituencies broken whilst the 1884-85 electoral reforms paved the way for Catholic Home Rule political dominance in most of Ireland between 1885 and 1918. Parnell's transformation of the Home Rule Party into a formidable expression of Irish discontent at Westminster coincided with the Land War of 1879-82 which undermined the position of the Irish landlords, many of whom were Protestant. New Unionist political initiatives in Ireland in 1885-86 hardened already serious divisions between the Irish Unionist and Nationalist communities.[5] The disestablishment of the Irish Anglican Church in 1869 did not fulfil Quaker hopes of better understanding between the religious communities in Ireland.[6]

Gladstone's support for Home Rule in 1886 changed the whole character of Anglo-Irish politics, for he upset the previously unquestioned British commitment to the Union as the foundation of Anglo-Irish relations and threatened the essential security the Union represented to the minority Protestant community. 1886 confronted Irish Protestants with the prospect of a Catholic Nationalist political majority, allied to an Ultramontane Roman Catholic Church, governing Ireland. The Protestant minority felt unable to trust the goodwill and understanding of the overwhelming Catholic majority. Fearful for their religious and economic status most Irish Quakers joined with their fellow Protestants in supporting the maintenance of the Union. Quaker responses to Gladstone's Home Rule Bills can be briefly outlined.

London Yearly Meeting expressed warm sympathy and prayerful support for Irish Friends in 1886 and 1893 but involved itself on neither occasion in public controversy.[7] It is clear however that the Home Rule Question caused serious divisions amongst British Friends. *The Friend* in 1890 declared that the Irish Question was 'a sore in our corporate life which is a source of great weakness'.[8] In 1893 the majority of British Friends appear to have supported Gladstone. The English Quaker Evangelical leader, J.Bevan Braithwaite, when addressing a conference of Unionist Friends in London in April 1893, declared: 'I earnestly trust that a matter of this sort will be entirely kept out of our Yearly Meeting . . . rather than that the unity of our Religious Society should be at all endangered'.[9] His words were heeded, but there was a Unionist minority amongst British Friends who by their vigorous support for the Union sustained their Irish co-religionists on both occasions. The most outstanding was John Bright, the Quaker Liberal politician. His refusal to support Gladstone in 1886 and his decision to vote against the second reading of the Bill encouraged sufficient Liberal dissident support to ensure defeat of the Bill in June 1886.[10] He died in 1889, but in 1893 there were other Friends whose activities at least encouraged the morale of Irish Friends. Foremost amongst them were the bankers J.H.Tuke and Thomas Hodgkin. Tuke had seen a decade's active concern for the social and economic condition of the West of Ireland recognised by his appointment to the Congested Districts Board in 1891.[11] Hodgkin brought to the Unionist cause a deep commitment to the Union and Irish Friends' well-being. His organisation of a Unionist Friends Conference in London, held on the same day that the Home Rule Bill received its second reading in the Commons, proved a successful if limited opportunity to express support for the Irish Friends' position.[12] Although out of membership for much of the Home Rule crisis the Gloucester printer John Bellows gave strong support both in the publication of Unionist pamphlets and the organisation of Unionist political meetings.[13] The activities of this Unionist minority may have compensated for what Irish Friends felt was the total incomprehension of the majority of British Friends as to what Home Rule meant for the Protestant community in Ireland.[14]

Irish Friends looked to British Friends for support in the crisis, a reflection of the larger Unionist dependence of the Irish Protestant community upon Britain in this issue. Prominent amongst Irish Quaker Unionists were the Pim family of Dublin[15] and the Richardson family of Bessbrook. In 1886 Dublin Yearly Meeting felt unable to take positive steps,[16] but in 1893 decisive action had been taken before the Yearly Meeting met. In March 1893 an Address was forwarded appealing to British Friends for support against the Home Rule Bill. It contained the signatures of 1,376 Quakers out of a total adult membership of 1,690 in Ireland.[17] More importantly Irish Quakers also forwarded a petition, with the signatures of 1,588 Friends and attenders, requesting the House of Commons not to pass the Bill. It was presented to the Commons by Bright's son, John Albert Bright, the Unionist Member for Central Birmingham.[18] A counter-address supporting Home Rule was issued over the signature of twenty-two Friends in April 1893, but its credibility was seriously questioned by James N.Richardson at the Unionist Friends Conference in London later that month.[19] Thus Home Rule in 1893 divided the two Quaker communities with an Irish Quaker majority opposing it and a British Quaker majority supporting it. The ensuing controversy produced pamphlets on both sides[20] but neither Yearly Meeting experienced it.

A new dimension had appeared for Irish Friends in the contentions Home Rule produced. Dublin Yearly Meeting on 6 May 1893 concentrated its discussion of the crisis on a minute of Ulster Quarterly Meeting, dated 20 March 1893.[21] Yearly Meeting united with its emphasis on maintaining the Friends' peace testimony during the crisis and commended this to 'Friends throughout Ireland'. The Yearly Meeting minute did not specifically mention Ulster, but during the discussion it was made clear that Ulster Friends faced being involved in a campaign of active resistance within that Province against the implementation of Home Rule. One Friend had already resigned from the Society due to the 'probability . . . of having to act in self-defence'. Other Friends believed they might be expected to undertake 'passive resistance'. The Ulster minute, in the aftermath of the Ulster Unionist Convention of 1892, sought Quaker unity in a situation which reflected essential differences in the composition and strength, as well as the regional character, of the two Unionist communities in Ireland. Friends did not however explore the possibility, present in 1893, of future separation between Ulster and the South. Friends were not alone in failing to perceive the full implications of what could happen,[22] but these were deferred by the Lords' defeat of Gladstone's Bill in September 1893.

The majority of Irish Quakers thus shared the basic Unionist response to Home Rule. This is understandable given that the circumstances in which Quakerism was introduced into Ireland made it Anglo-Irish in cultural identity. With Home Rule Quakers found themselves part of two Unionist communities in Ireland, that in the South dominated by the old Anglican Ascendancy landed class and in the North by the Ulster Presbyterians. Their total response reflected a Unionist awareness of a lack of effective integration within much of Ireland, regardless of past contributions. Irish Friends had identified themselves with the cause of equal civil and religious rights in Ireland, especially Roman Catholic Emancipation and Irish Anglican Church Disestablishment.[23] Quaker disappointment at increasing religious and political division in Ireland after 1869 was expressed decisively in 1886 and 1893. In part this also expressed a Quaker sense of loss of a positive role they had previously undertaken in Irish society. The Home Rule controversy destroyed years of patient effort on the part of many Irish Friends to promote better understanding between Catholic and Protestant. These had included respect for Catholic neighbours and a refusal to associate with Protestant extremism in the North; John Grubb Richardson's development of Bessbrook; some Quaker support, notably Richardson and Bright, for non-sectarian education and the Quaker commitment to religious equality.[24] Quaker neutrality was now buried under major religious and political differences.

Home Rule Friends generously but vainly urged their co-religionists to 'trust their fellow countrymen' and to work together for improved Anglo-Irish relations through Irish majority wishes. They could not however deny the divisions which accompanied the prospect of Home Rule and they underestimated the real depth of fear the Protestant community felt at being subject to a Catholic-dominated Irish state.[25] Unionist Friends saw their fears realised in Catholic press-statements that the two communities could not 'freely co-exist in the same society'.[26] The considerable damage Ireland suffered in the controversies surrounding the fall of Parnell, the consequent division of the Home Rule Party, and the County Meath electoral petitions of 1892[27] strengthened their adherence to the Union. Most Irish Friends concluded that their commitment to 'equal liberties and equal opportunities for all creeds and all parties' rested within a Union which was 'the common property of the people of Ireland'. Moreover the 'moderating, regularising force'[28] of the Union held a balance in the tensions between the Catholic and Protestant communities which so disturbed Friends. To maintain the Union however meant closer links with Britain at the expense of the constitutional alternative the largely Catholic majority had electorally favoured. This clash of aspirations further distanced the two communities whilst the Home Rule majority did nothing to allay the minority's fears.

Quaker standing in Irish society rested largely on their economic success in the business community. Quaker businessmen believed that Home Rule would undermine economic confidence and stability, ruin trade and create large-scale unemployment. This led Tuke, J.N.Richardson and Hodgkin to argue that the Catholic majority was politically, administratively and economically unfit to manage Irish affairs.[29] It was here that disparagement of the Catholic majority became most marked. Friends' forthright expression of their business expertise implied a Protestant monopoly in an economic contest while their dismissal of majority aspirations ignored basic Irish electoral facts.[30] Friends came closest to emulating eighteenth-century Anglican Ascendancy attitudes in expressing their belief that the Protestant community contained all that was best and indispensable to Irish well-being.[31] These sentiments were common stock in Unionist arguments and were products of a situation of considerable stress. Such attitudes were a reminder of the impossibility of compromise in the Home Rule issue.

In 1893 Quakers under-played their Irish identity whilst their petition to the House of Commons indisputably placed them with the Unionist community in Ireland. Quakers were however caught in the tragic dilemma facing the Anglo-Irish community. Many loved Ireland[32] but felt closest to Britain and could not resolve the tension this created. For most fundamentally Irish Quaker responses to Home Rule were part of the conflict of cultures described by F.S.L.Lyons in his Ford Lectures of 1978.[33] He identified this conflict as a prime factor in the failure of Anglo-Irish relations under the Union. Quakers found themselves involved, as members of the Anglo-Irish and Ulster communities, in the deep clash between the English and the Gaelic cultural traditions. With the latter they had effectively little in common. New depths were added to already considerable community divisions when Irish cultural tensions surfaced with decisive force between 1891 and 1916.

English and Irish Quakers had moved from the unity within the Quaker communities in 1846, which had made effective famine relief initiatives possible, to disunity between 1886 and 1893 over the issue of future Irish development. The pressure of the Home Rule crisis resulted in Irish Quakers being no longer able to stand apart from conflicting community aspirations in Ireland.[34]

NOTES

[1] Isabel Grubb, *Quakers in Ireland, 1654-1900* (London, 1927), pp. 16-17.
[2] *Ibid.*, pp. 73-79, 139-42.
[3] The following paragraph is based on: J.C.Beckett, *The Making of Modern Ireland, 1603-1923* (London, 1966), pp. 280-91; Oliver MacDonagh, *Ireland: The Union and its Aftermath* (London, 1977), pp. 13-32; T.W.Moody, *Davitt and Irish Revolution, 1846-82* (Oxford, 1981), pp. 25-27; P.O'Farrell, *England and Ireland since 1800* (Oxford, 1979), p. 29.
[4] J.C.Beckett, *The Anglo-Irish Tradition* (Belfast, 1983), p. 89; Conor Cruise O'Brien (ed.), *The Shaping of Modern Ireland* (London, 1970), p. 1.
[5] Patrick Buckland, *Irish Unionism 1: The Anglo-Irish and the New Ireland, 1885-1922* (Dublin, 1972), pp. 1-6.
[6] Friends Historical Collection, Dublin, PB 9/12, F.W.Pim, *The Society of Friends and Home Rule* (Dublin, 1893), p. 18; Friends House Library, London, Tract Volume 382, no. 30, Anne Richardson, *Two Irish Members of the Society of Friends on the Irish Question* (Gloucester, 1893), p. 6.
[7] *The British Friend* (Glasgow), vol. 44, 6 Month 1, 1886, p. 114; *Ibid.*, (Birkenhead), New Series, vol. 2, 6 Month, 1893; p. 141.
[8] Elizabeth Isichei, *Victorian Quakers* (Oxford, 1970), p. 201.
[9] Friends Historical Collection, Dublin, PB 9/13, *Conference of Friends Upon the Home Rule Question... 21 April 1893* (hereafter cited as *Friends Conference... 1893*), pp. 5-9.
[10] R.A.J.Walling (ed.), *The Diaries of John Bright* (London, 1930), pp. 541-43.
[11] Sir Edward Fry, *James Hack Tuke, A Memoir* (London, 1899), *passim.*
[12] Friends House Library, London, Tract Volume 382, no. 29, Thomas Hodgkin, *The Two Rules: Home Rule and the Golden Rule* (Gloucester, 1893), *passim;* Louise Creighton, *Life and Letters of Thomas Hodgkin* (London, 1917), pp. 162-63; Friends Historical Collection, Dublin, PB 21/96, *To Our Fellow Members of the Religious Society of Friends in Ireland, April 1893.*
[13] John Bellows, *Letters and Memoir* (London, 1904), pp. 61-69, 101-02. He also spoke at the Unionist Friends Conference.
[14] See e.g. Pim, *op. cit.*, pp. 16-17, 20-21; Anne Richardson, *op. cit.*, pp. 11-16.
[15] Buckland, *op. cit.*, p. 18.

[16] *The British Friend* (Glasgow), vol. 44, 6 Month 1, 1886, pp. 146-47, 149.

[17] Pim, *op. cit.*, pp. 5-7.

[18] Friends Historical Collection, Dublin, PB 21/98, *Petition Form; Friends Conference . . . 1893*, p. 47.

[19] Friends Historical Collection, Dublin, PB 21/97, *Nationalist Friends Address*, 1893; Friends House Library, London, Tract Volume 382, no. 30, J.N.Richardson, *Two Irish Members of the Society of Friends on the Irish Question* (Gloucester, 1893), pp. 3-4. See also Pim, *op. cit.*, pp. 22-24.

[20] In addition to those already cited, for a pro Home Rule view see Friends Historical Collection, Dublin, PB 21/95, W. Martin Wood, *Home Rule and the Society of Friends* (London, 1893).

[21] *The British Friend*, (Birkenhead), New Series, vol. 2, 6 Month, 1893, pp. 157-58.

[22] Buckland, *op. cit.*, p. 17; Charles Townshend, *Political Violence in Ireland* (Oxford, 1983), pp. 191-92.

[23] Anne Richardson, *op. cit.*, p. 6.

[24] Pim, *op. cit.*, pp. 16-17; Anne Richardson, *op. cit.*, pp. 6-8; J.M.R., *Six Generations of Friends in Ireland, 1655-1890* (London, 1893), pp. 150-51, and chapter VII, *passim*.

[25] *Nationalist Friends Address*, 1893, especially Points 4, 6 and 7; Wood, *op. cit.*, passim.

[26] Anne Richardson, *op. cit.*, p. 14.

[27] Pim, *op. cit.*, pp. 18-20; C.J.Woods, 'The General Election of 1892: the Catholic Clergy and the defeat of the Parnellites', in F.S.L.Lyons and R.A.J.Hawkins (ed.), *Ireland Under the Union* (Oxford, 1980), especially pp. 297-302, 311-12.

[28] Pim, *op. cit.*, pp. 18, 23.

[29] Fry, *op. cit.*, pp. 226-28; J.N.Richardson, *op. cit.*, pp. 1-3; Hodgkin, *op. cit.*, p. 7.

[30] *Conference of Friends . . . 1893*, p. 49.

[31] Hodgkin, *op. cit.*, p. 7; Anne Richardson, *op. cit.*, p. 16.

[32] Anne Richardson, *op. cit.*, p. 16.

[33] F.S.L.Lyons, *Culture and Anarchy in Ireland 1890-1939* (Oxford, 1979), chapters I-V, *passim*.

[34] Desmond Bowen, *The Protestant Crusade in Ireland 1800-70* (Dublin, 1978), pp. 38-39, 302-04.

WRITTEN EPISTLES OF LONDON YEARLY MEETING IN THE EIGHTEENTH CENTURY

by David J. Hall

Twelve years ago, on notionally completing a study of the development of the discipline of the Society of Friends from 1738 to 1861, I became aware of several questions unanswered there. One of the more manageable was the reason for the existence of a series of epistles issued in manuscript, in parallel with the well-known printed epistle issued throughout the eighteenth century by London Yearly Meeting. This theme was followed up with the encouragement of Edward Milligan. In the intervening years I have been reminded occasionally that the results were not yet available. The present occasion seems an appropriate one to reveal them.

The annual printed epistle containing its combination of report, exhortation and advice was issued after the Yearly Meeting had completed its business. In a number of years in the eighteenth century there was issued in addition a written epistle, so described in the minutes of Yearly Meeting, in the minutes of the meeting receiving the epistle, and in the books of discipline quoting from it. It was customary also for the Yearly Meeting to send out advices in writing on particular subjects. In most cases these can be distinguished easily from the written epistles which are more general in content and more formal in arrangement, but in a few cases referred to below the distinction is blurred. The written epistles discussed here are only those sent out to (at least) all the quarterly meetings of Friends in England. Many other manuscript epistles were sent out by the

Yearly Meeting to the other yearly meetings whose epistles were received or on occasion to individual meetings in this country.[1]

It is relatively straightforward to establish the number of written epistles. It is less clear why they were issued. Other connected questions arise: as to how far their content was related to that of the parallel printed epistle; as to how far they were, or were not, expected to reach exactly the same audience; as to how extensively the books of discipline quoted from them, and as to whether any pattern can be detected to explain their issue in particular years.

At first sight there appear to be nineteen written epistles from the eighteenth century. These may be identified by the presence of their texts in the minutes of Yearly Meeting, or by quotations in the books of discipline, for the following years: 1715, 1718, 1731, 1736, 1737, 1743, 1745, 1750, 1751, 1752, 1753, 1755, 1760, 1774, 1786, 1790, 1792, 1795 and 1798. Two of them, those for 1786 and 1798, initially present problems because their text cannot be found in the minutes of Yearly Meeting; four others, 1715, 1718, 1731 and 1755 are to be found there, but may be incorrectly described.

The first problem epistle can be dismissed easily: it is the result of a misprint in the source which appears to quote from it and in fact comes from the ordinary, printed epistle for 1786.[2] The second problem epistle for 1798 is referred to in the minutes of Yearly Meeting for 1799 thus:

> This Committee, on taking into consideration the answers to the queries, is of the judgment that it will be useful to call the attention of quarterly meetings to the subjects of the written epistle of last year, and that they be desired to report to the next Yearly Meeting, what care has been taken respecting the same.[3]

It can be found in the minutes of the London and Middlesex Quarterly Meeting.[4] In form it is similar to the written epistles discussed below although concerned entirely with one subject, the broad one of 'the state of our Society, as represented in the Answers to the Queries'. The epistle is, as usual, signed 'in and on behalf of the Yearly Meeting, held in London' and presumably its omission from the Yearly Meeting minutes for 1798 was due to oversight on the part of the Clerk.

The written epistle for 1715 falls somewhere between the class of definite and doubtful written epistles. The extract in the second book of discipline[5] identified as coming from the written epistle for 1715 comes in fact from a section of the Yearly Meeting minutes for that year described as 'some written minutes of this meeting to be sent to the counties'.[6] These written minutes are without the normal preamble found to the other written epistles discussed below, and they cover also a number of subjects.

Apart from the absence of the preamble the 1715 epistle does seem to fit into the general category.

The written epistles for 1718, 1731 and 1755, although of a length similar to the other written epistles, are concerned each entirely with one subject. Those for 1718 and 1731 are described in the second book of discipline as written epistles. That for 1718 is entitled 'An Epistle of Caution brought in against the Growing Evil of Pride' and was brought into the Yearly Meeting by the Committee appointed to draw up the printed epistle.[7] The Yearly Meeting directed that it was to be sent to the quarterly meetings and monthly meetings 'in order to be sent to every Family of Friends'.[8] Both the 1718 and 1731 written epistles are rather wide-ranging in their treatment of their subject, so that the 1718 epistle is quoted under three different headings in the 1783 book of discipline. The 1731 written epistle is 'an Epistle to the Countys in manuscript of advice for Friends who travel'.[9] This is described by the minutes of Yearly Meeting as a written epistle, a copy was to be sent to 'each County, and also to North Britain, and Ireland with all convenient expedition'.

The written epistle for 1755 is again strictly speaking a minute, concerned with one subject, the holding of weekday meetings.[10] It was brought into the Yearly Meeting from the committee appointed to draw up the epistle and is not referred to as a written epistle in those minutes.[11] The minutes of the London and Middlesex Quarterly Meeting contain the text without referring to it as a written epistle.[12] However the minutes of Swarthmore Monthly Meeting report that 'The Written Epistle from the Yearly Meeting held in London was brought to this meeting and Copies thereof sent to the Sundry Meetings'.[13] The confusion is understandable; a contemporary annotation 'Epistles or Minutes to be sent in Mss' in Yearly Meeting minutes adjacent to an entry reporting that Joseph Fry has brought in 'the following Minute . . .', illustrates the close relation between minutes and epistles.[14]

The attempt to draw a clear distinction between the written epistles and extended minutes of advice may be unwise. Another example may be quoted of a minute that could easily have been called a written epistle by the compilers of a book of a discipline, or the clerk of an inferior meeting in writing a marginal note in his minute book. The minute on tithe in 1706 was to be sent out in manuscript with the printed epistle from the Yearly Meeting, in the normal fashion in which many minutes reached quarterly meetings, although there is seldom any reference to the specific method of transmission in the minutes of Yearly Meeting.[15]

The written epistle for 1774[16] is also concerned entirely with one subject, calm at the time of an approaching general election, but in every other way it satisfies the criteria set out here for other written epistles, unlike that for 1775. The minutes of Yearly Meeting refer to it as one of the two epistles brought in from 'the Committee appointed to prepare an Epistle or Epistles', 'which being several times read, was with some Alterations, agreed to, and written Copies are to be sent to the several Counties and places in Great Britain.' But the minutes of the London and Middlesex Quarterly Meeting describe this epistle as a minute, showing again that there is a certain arbitrariness in any attempt to define the written epistles too precisely.[17]

This confusion about the difference between minutes and epistles is not sufficient to explain away the existence of a separate epistle circulated in manuscript in some years of the eighteenth century and there is little help in the minutes of Yearly Meeting. We are told by the relevant minute in 1743 that the committee appointed to draw up the epistle had provided 'also one to be sent in Manuscript to the several Quarterly Meetings . . .'[18] In 1736 and 1737 there was some further indication of the purpose of the written epistle. In 1736 the committee to draw up the epistle were told 'It's also Refer'd to them to Draw up a written Epistle relating to some advices not so Proper to be Published in print'.[19] In 1737, less clearly, the committee reported back that they 'thought proper to communicate several things to Friends by a Written Epistle . . .'[20] At the beginning of the next century the purpose and form of the Yearly Meeting's epistles was described comprehensively in Clarkson's *Portraiture of Quakerism:*

> This letter usually comprehends three subjects: first, the State of the Society; in which the sufferings for tithes and other demands of the church are included. This state, in all its different branches, the committee ascertain by inspecting the answers, as brought by the deputies before mentioned.
>
> A second subject, comprehended in the letter, is Advice to the Society for the Regulation of their moral and civil Conduct.—This advice is suggested partly from the same written answers, and partly by the circumstances of the times. Are there, for instance, any vicious customs creeping into the Society, or any new dispositions among its members contrary to the Quaker-principles? . . . New admonitions and advices follow.
>
> A third subject, comprehended in the letter, and which I believe since the year 1787 has frequently formed a standing article in it, is the Slave-Trade . . . These, and occasionally other subjects, having been duly weighed by the committee, they begin to compose the letter.
>
> When the letter is ready, it is brought into the public meeting, and the whole of it, without interruption is first read audibly. It is then

read over again, and canvassed sentence by sentence. Every sentence, nay every word, is liable to alteration; for any one may make his remarks, and nothing can stand but by the sense of the meeting. When finally settled and approved, it is printed, and dispersed among the members throughout the nation. This letter may be considered as informing the Society of certain matters that occurred in the preceding year, and as conveying to them admonitions on various subjects. This letter is emphatically styled 'The General Epistle'.[21]

Clarkson's account of the preparation of the General Epistle, at least up to the time of its being ordered to be printed, must apply equally to the preparation of the written epistle by the same Committee. However, he does not mention the existence of the written epistles. The written epistles seem to perform much the same function as the 'General Epistle' described in his penultimate sentence. Perhaps the chief difference is in the degree of intimacy involved rather than in emphasis. It is probable that the written epistles were not intended to go at all beyond the audience to whom they were addressed, while the printed epistle, circulated in increasing numbers throughout the century, represented the public face of the Society and could, if need be, be used as evidence of the Society's concerns and attitudes.

Assessment of the impact of the written epistles appears to be impossible. While a survey of a large sample of quarterly or monthly meeting records when the written epistles were received might provide some clue, this is not particularly likely. In the books of discipline it is at least possible to see what parts of the epistles were thought to have a more general or lasting application. In the copy of the 1738 book examined (it had been kept up-to-date to 1760)[22] there were fifteen quotations from the written epistles. There were thirty-one quotations, of which only two came from years after 1760, in the first printed book of discipline in 1783.

The texts of the printed epistles of Yearly Meeting are readily available in published collections[23] as well as in their individual printed versions, and it seems useful for purposes of comparison to give here a summary of the contents of the written epistles with a note of their location in the minutes of Yearly Meeting. The summary indicates also where a particular theme is covered both in the printed and written epistles for any year.

1715 Minutes of Yearly Meeting, Volume v, pp. 126-30
a) Recommends further attention to written minute of 1713 on affirmation.
b) Friends to be careful to attend meetings for worship and discipline.
c) Trustees and executors to be conscientious.

d) No monthly meeting to divide itself without the consent and concurrence of the quarterly meeting.

e) The behaviour of the young, plainness. (Also in printed epistle, subsequently PE.)

1736 Volume VIII, pp. 248-51

a) Tithe (also in PE), abortive bill to relieve Friends from persecution for not paying.

b) The Society's need for funds.

c) A proposal to print accounts of sufferings on account of tithes.

d) Too many appeals reaching the Yearly Meeting.

e) Urging attendance at meetings for discipline (also in PE).

f) Young ministers to be encouraged.

1737 Volume VIII, pp. 329-32

a) Need to secure title deeds of properties.

b) Printing of records of sufferings.

c) Encouragement of learning foreign languages.

d) Re-admission to membership not necessarily indicating the acceptability of ministry.

e) Concern caused by questions of tithe and bad debts.

f) Contributions to collections from those who have failed in business not acceptable.

g) Differences to be settled privately or through arbitrators rather than through monthly or quarterly meetings or at law.

1743 Volume IX, pp. 164-68

a) Dealing with offenders; the problems caused when offences were not reproved and then objections were raised at the time of marriage.

b) Elders to encourage attention to the discipline in the young (specific reference to the PE).

c) Declension from simplicity.

d) The need for plainness of speech without respect of persons.

e) Care in appointing elders and representatives.

f) Requirements for testimonies of public Friends deceased.

1745 Volume IX, pp. 309-12

a) Meetings to ask for certificates of those travelling in the ministry.

b) None to offer themselves as preachers if not found clear on the testimonies, e.g. tithe.

c) Encouraging the service of women in meetings.

d) The example to be given by teachers.

e) Friends not to wear mourning.

1750 Volume x, pp. 221-24
a) An apparent reduction in sufferings thought perhaps to be due to a want of care in recording.
b) Changing practices in claiming of church rates and tithes.
c) Run goods.
d) General points on discipline.

1751 Volume x, pp. 299-303
a) Satisfaction with answer to Queries.
b) Education—difficulties of children educated by teachers who are not Friends.
c) General care of children.
d) Exhortation to elders.

1752 Volume x, pp. 375-77
a) Watching against strife and division.
b) Discretion of Friends travelling in ministry.
c) Joining together small monthly meetings where necessary.
d) Appointment of overseers.
e) Tithe.

1753 Volume x, pp. 461-65
a) Fear that answers to Queries are unduly optimistic, neglect of Advices.
b) All monthly meetings and quarterly meetings to have the 1718 Advice on plainness read.
c) Example to be given by parents.
d) Care of apprentices.
e) Convincement.
f) Care by elders for youth called to the ministry.
g) Example of 'ancients' in diligent attendance at meetings.
h) Elders and overseers to be careful of their reputations.

1760 Volume xii, pp. 105-08
a) Substitutes in the militia.
b) The sorrowful state of the church and need for strengthening of discipline.
c) Answers to Queries to be plain and explicit.

1774 Volume xv, pp. 129-31
Advising calm in the time of an approaching general election, avoiding intemperance and corruption.

1790 Volume XVIII, pp. 598-604

a) Need for a better adherence to discipline.

b) Neglect in answers to the 7th Query, about setting a good example, particularly in reading of scripture and in 'plainness of speech, behaviour, and apparel'.

c) Testimony against tithes.

d) Evasion of revenue duties.

e) Right attitudes to an approaching general election. (Also in PE.)

f) Enquiries to be made where it appears that Friends may be concerned in bearing or manufacturing arms, hiring out ships.

g) Visiting those moving in by certificate.

h) Visiting meetings appearing weak.

1792 Volume XIX, pp. 126-27

a) Duty of admonition.

b) Visiting monthly meetings.

1795 Volume XIX, pp. 265-71

a) Signs of improvement in answers to Queries.

b) Management of discipline not to be in unclean hands.

c) Warning against vain sports, leisure to be devoted to the service of neighbours.

d) Tithe.

e) Deficiencies in observing the testimony on war.

1798 Volume XIII of the minutes of London and Middlesex Quarterly Meeting, pp. 24-27

a) Deficiencies in the answers to Queries, especially on neglect of meetings for worship, religious education.

b) Quarterly meetings to assist monthly meetings.

c) Friends to keep to the words of a Query in answering it.

NOTES

The preparation of this study was helped very much by discussions with Edward H. Milligan and by comments made by Russell S. Mortimer on an earlier version.

[1] See the manuscript record 'Epistles Sent' in ten volumes at Friends House Library.

[2] *Appendix to the Extracts from the Minutes and Advices of the Yearly Meeting of Friends held in London* (London, 1792), p. 1.

[3] Minutes of London Yearly Meeting (hereafter YMM), volume XIX, p. 444. At Friends House Library.

[4] Volume XIII, pp. 24-27. At Friends House Library.

5 *Extracts from the Minutes and Advices of the Yearly Meeting of Friends held in London* (London, 1783).

6 YMM, volume v, p. 126.

7 YMM, volume v, pp. 305-10.

8 YMM, volume v, p. 310.

9 YMM, volume vii, pp. 269-73.

10 YMM, volume xi, pp. 83-85.

11 YMM, volume xi, p. 84.

12 Volume vi, pp. 52-57. At Friends House Library.

13 Volume xxv, unnumbered pages, entry for 29th. of 8mo. 1775. At Friends House Library.

14 YMM, volume xi, p. 83.

15 YMM, volume iii, p. 268.

16 YMM, volume xv, pp. 129-31.

17 Volume viii, pp. 220-22. At Friends House Library.

18 YMM, volume ix, p. 164.

19 YMM, volume viii, p. 245.

20 YMM, volume viii, p. 328.

21 T. Clarkson, *A Portraiture of Quakerism* (1806), volume i, pp. 242-44.

22 Christian and Brotherly Advices given forth from time to time by the Yearly Meetings in London (1738), manuscript. A large number of copies was issued.

23 The printed epistles were issued separately from 1682. Before that date the Yearly Meeting epistle was circulated in manuscript. A volume of extracts from the epistles for the period 1706-1731 was published in York, *c*.1732. Four collected editions may be noted:

    i. *1675-1759* (with index), London, 1760.

    ii. *1675-1805*, Baltimore, 1806.

    iii. *1681-1817* (with introduction), York, 1818, or New York, 1821.

    iv. *1681-1857* (with an historical introduction and some earlier epistles), two volumes, London 1858.

GOD AT LONDON YEARLY MEETING 1900

by Hope Hewison

There is a story going round in Quaker circles about an elderly woman Friend who died at the close of Yearly Meeting. When asked by God in his heaven whether she had been a religious person on earth she replied, 'Oh yes! I'm a Quaker. I've just come from Yearly Meeting.' 'Dang it!' exclaimed the Lord thumping his knee, 'I knew there was somewhere I should have been last week!'

If it was London Yearly Meeting in 1900 that God had clean forgotten to attend, Friends had not forgotten him; they had, in fact, spent most of one session arguing about him. Apart from the nice question as to whether it is humanly possible to talk about God behind his back, I think it is more likely that God was there all the time, with his head in his hands during the two Peace sessions, quoting Shakespeare at himself, 'Lord! What fools these mortals be!' But, to continue for a moment in this anthropomorphic vein, I think it even more likely that the God whose love is wisdom was as prepared as ever to let his Quaker children find their own way home, believing in them and indeed in all his children always more deeply than they have ever believed in him.

It was, however, this very question of the relationship between God and his children, and who exactly were his children, that had been exercising and dividing Friends during the morning session on 31 May at Devonshire House. Nowhere in the official, traditionally composed *Extracts from the Minutes and Proceedings* that year is there any hint of theological crisis. This is not surprising for the regular work of the Society has to go on and be duly recorded despite changing winds of doctrine and temporary turbulence.

There are, however, numerous references to the cause of the turbulence and, in addition to such subjects considered as birthright membership, assistance to the Doukhobortsi, the duties of overseers, military service in Norway, the tabular statement and Solway Fishery membership, there was the Boer War, which had broken out seven months before and which was affecting the life of the whole nation including the Society of Friends.

Embedded in the pious phraseology of the Epistle there is mention of 'those in our own and other communities whose hearts are bowed under the burden of the present awful war'. The Report of the Peace Committee refers more explicitly to the war fever raging the country; it admits that while many Friends had done all in their power to oppose and protest against the present deplorable war others had felt unable to uphold actively the testimony against *all* war, and that on two occasions the Meeting for Sufferings had not seen its way to adopt the Committee's suggestions for public action. The summary of proceedings of the Meeting for Sufferings refers to its attempts to avert war and, like the Peace Committee's Report, mentions the issue in January 1900 of an abbreviated and altered version of the Peace Appeal published in 1854 during the Crimean War. There is the text of a short minute to be sent immediately to the Government and of the Peace Address to the nation finally approved by Yearly Meeting under the title 'Christianity and War'. Both are masterpieces of composition though the latter is very long—nearly five pages—and larded with scriptural references—fifteen of them—and quotations from John Bright, George Fox, Joseph Sturge, Milton, Wordsworth and Tertullian.

For all that, however, there is little to indicate how sorely the war was testing Friends' principles regarding peace or how the strain showed itself in disagreement regarding small side issues related to the war and in the serious controversy which erupted during Yearly Meeting about the Fatherhood of God. It is in the ample pages of *The Friend* and *The British Friend* that we can see how these internal dissensions developed, how they were interrelated and what God had to do with it all, even with the substitution of the name of Caleb R. Kemp for that of Joshua Rowntree on the committee appointed to see the Peace Address through the final stage of its preparation (*Y.M. Proc.*, 1900, p. 63). The first of the two Peace sessions took place on 23 May. It had before it the Peace Committee's Report and minutes from three quarterly meetings, two calling for public action against the war and one for renewed emphasis on the testimony against all war. The Clerk of Yearly Meeting that year, John Morland, suggested that all these documents be taken together. He told Friends he trusted the very canopy of peace might be over them and that their hearts and desires might be knit together in the bonds of peace. He did not go as far as the Clerk of Dublin Yearly Meeting had done earlier in the month when he not only prayed for peace in the gathering but also trusted that no attempt would be made to go into the political aspect of the question 'for with that,' he said, 'we as a Religious Society have nothing to do'. The apprehensions of both clerks, however, were well founded. J.Marshall Sturge of Berks and Oxon Quarterly Meeting, one of the two urging public action, brought the documents to the attention of London Yearly Meeting. He did so in no uncertain terms referring to the loss of individual liberty, the number of Friends who had put flags in their windows on the relief of Mafeking and those who seemed to support bloodshed in South Africa; Friends should either give up membership or be faithful to one of the greatest testimonies the world had ever had; they should memorialise Government for armistice and arbitration. William Charles Braithwaite, who followed, recognised that these were differences of interpretation of principle but felt there was no basic unsoundness. He proposed the appointment of a strong committee to prepare a minute to Government and a document for wider distribution restating the Christian testimony against war.

These two proposals were accepted but not before over twenty Friends had expressed themselves on the matter, many welcoming the proposals, some giving vent to their feelings about the war, two referring to England's bad name on the Continent; one, Ellen Robinson, insisting that Friends were not judging others as people but condemning their actions; and Howard Nicholson feeling it would be better for us to be defeated looking at the moral after-effects of a successful war against a nation of farmers. It was Edward Grubb who brought God out of the wings and on to the stage in this session. He felt Quakers were treating the war too traditionally and not as springing from the fundamental principles of true Quakerism. He hoped Yearly Meeting would suggest in its testimony that their foundation of thought rested on the Universal Fatherhood of God made known to us in Jesus Christ and the presence in each one of his children whom his hands had fashioned of a portion of his divine spirit; if we all believed in this rather than relying on isolated texts of Scripture we should be more effective in reaching the hearts and minds of those we wished to influence. After a little more of this the Clerk reminded him that time was too short for long speeches. More Friends were now emboldened to speak. Caleb R.Kemp hoped Friends would not turn aside into anything that had the colour of politics; that sort of thing should be left to the politicians and statesmen. Some Friends were not happy about memorialising the Government; others, including Joseph Storrs Fry, were not happy about going into details on which Quakers were divided.

Finally a minute was approved separating a committee to prepare the two documents. It was indeed strong, consisting of nineteen members including Ellen Robinson, Frances Thompson, William C.Braithwaite, John E.Wilson, Joshua Rowntree, J.Marshall Sturge, Thomas P.Newman, John Stephenson Rowntree, Joan M.Fry and both Caleb R.Kemp and Edward Grubb.

On 25 May John Stephenson Rowntree introduced the review of the state of the Society. He deplored the habit of being hopeful and joyful in Yearly Meeting epistles whatever happened. Never at any time had there been greater sorrow and anxiety, with famine and plague in India and the panorama of hell in South Africa. He spoke of England intoxicated by war and jingoistic patriotism, and the loss of free speech so that the rich man with his *Times* and the poor man with his *Daily Mail* were not finding spiritual sustenance. He reminded Friends of the sufferings of early Friends and the way they had been silenced at their prison windows by the beating of drums; everything depended on how we held up in times of unpopularity the truth of God. 'He who fights for England fights for God' was a return to the old tribal concept of God. Friends bore a special responsibility to the Christian Church. The official minute translated all this into more conventional religious phraseology: 'We desire that Friends may be strengthened to be faithful even unto death, that they may receive the crown of life'.

Friends met again, pursuant to adjournment, on 31 May to consider the two documents prepared by the drafting committee. Before they began to do this, Howard Nicholson spoke by permission of the Clerk and spoke at length. He deplored the tendency to political considerations in Friends' agitation about stopping the war; this lowered our testimony against *all* war by excusing or condemning a particular war on special grounds. He was distressed about the newspaper controversy which had led people to ask whether Quakers themselves were not divided (*Reynolds Newspaper* had said that the sect was no longer to be regarded as a strenuous peace organisation) and this had put them in danger of becoming a laughing stock; he condemned both pulpit and press for cultivating the war spirit, Quaker MPs in voting monetary payment to a man (Lord Roberts) who had come back from a heathen land with his sword red with human blood, and he protested against a pamphlet, *The South African War*, which strongly commended certain statesmen to the Society. (Albert J.Crosfield later assured Friends that this had been published without the authority of the Meeting for Sufferings and had not been paid for out of the National Stock.) He assailed Ellen Robinson (it was in fact Frances Thompson) for having said that some non-Christians had higher standards than ourselves and that the question of peace was not a question first of conversion. At this point the Clerk asked him not to introduce personalities. Howard

Nicholson continued, saying he failed to see any Kingdom of Peace on earth except by the coming of the Son of Man. He welcomed different views among Friends on such subjects as birthright membership but not on theological questions, and he criticised invertebrate Quakers who looked on traditional principles as mere prejudices.

The Clerk now called the attention of Yearly Meeting to the two draft documents. The appeal to Government, in short, minute form, presented little difficulty and was soon accepted. John E. Wilson asked Friends to note that there was a marked absence of detail in both this and the next document, not because of differences on the committee, which had, to his surprise, been absolutely unanimous.

The draft Peace Address was then read by William C. Braithwaite. Howard Nicholson (this is attributed to Herbert Nicholson but in the context of the argument it seems it should be Howard) rose almost immediately to object to the phrase 'the Fatherhood of God', as if God were the father of everyone. He was the creator of everyone but the father of those who had given their hearts to him. His objection was supported by William Henry Wilson and on several occasions by a number of unnamed Friends. Howard Nicholson rose again to say he believed that the 'Fatherhood of God and the Brotherhood of Man' were utterly out of harmony with New Testament teaching. Other Friends hoped the document would go out unabridged; among these were John Bellows, Henrietta Brown, William Noble, Frances Thompson, William Hobson and, expressing astonishment that anyone should object to the concept of the Fatherhood of God, Howard Hodgkin and John Stephenson Rowntree.

Again Howard Nicholson spoke, this time disagreeing with another passage in the address, that we became the children of God by loving our enemies; we loved our enemies, he declared, because we were the children of God. He had also been astonished, but in his case because the majority of Friends present were willing to trample on the weaker consciences of their brethren. Albert J. Crosfield quoted 'Love your enemies . . . that you may be the children of your Father which is in Heaven'. There were yet others, like Eliza Richardson, who wanted modification of the wording for the sake of Friends in Ireland, or who pleaded for charity with the views of the minority, or who hoped the circulation of the document would not be limited by the retention of what was objected to. Joseph Storrs Fry hoped there would be some modification in view of the large expression of opinion to this effect. An unnamed Irish Friend, while personally concurring with the doctrines contained in the words, thought it very desirable to avoid strife by omitting them. At this point, after more than thirty contributions, the Clerk ruled that the words should be omitted.

Even as Johannesburg was being captured by the British and the Transvaal Government was fleeing—though the end of the war was still two years away—Friends had been locked in theological controversy on the Fatherhood of God, with two other elements influencing the eventual outcome of the debate, those who believed in it as a doctrine but felt it would be better not to mention it in the Peace Address, and those like William C. Braithwaite who felt that the implication of it in the rest of the document was more important than explicit reference. And it was William C. Braithwaite who appeared to have the last word. While accepting the alteration, the thought being really contained in the rest of the Address, he hoped it would not go forth that Friends did not believe in the Fatherhood of God and the Brotherhood of Man.

The Clerk then read a minute accepting the document as modified. But all was still not quite over. Joshua Rowntree expressed his desire to withdraw from the committee of three Friends—the others were William C. Braithwaite and Thomas P. Newman—appointed to revise the document and see to its distribution. C.C. Morland and many others appealed to him to continue, the alteration being the wish of only a few. Joshua Rowntree still felt unable to do so. The Clerk said it was not a matter of principle at stake; if it had been he would not have ruled as he had done. The name of John Stephenson Rowntree was put forward instead but he too declined; the omission to him struck at the very foundation of the argument in the document. William C. Braithwaite repeated his conviction that the doctrine was still there by implication; it would not otherwise have been worth sending out. John E. Wilson thought it was a most serious step for Yearly Meeting as a whole to excise it. Frederick Cash and many others wanted the words restored. Richard R. Fox thought it a most dangerous precedent to do this after the Clerk's ruling. Albert J. Crosfield and Charles Brady agreed, though the latter believed the excision was a serious and retrograde step. So did Thomas Pumphrey adding that the Friends who had urged it would have to bear a heavy responsibility. William C. Braithwaite agreed with Richard R. Fox but hoped that those Friends who had pressed for the omission would see that others were also prepared to give up a good deal in the cause of peace. Joseph Storrs Fry concurred. Howard Nicholson said he had been entirely misunderstood by the meeting. The name of Caleb R. Kemp was substituted for that of Joshua Rowntree. The Peace Address in its final form was brought to the last session of Yearly Meeting the next morning. The Clerk felt impelled to say a few words to remove the weight resting on their minds regarding the removal of a paragraph from the document. He explained lovingly and carefully that this had not represented a denial of the truth; it was in condescension to the minority that it had been done and the words omitted had been part of an argument still contained in the document. He quoted many texts and, in conclusion, urged Friends to cast their burdens on the Lord. Joseph Storrs Fry, as one who had sat at the table for many years, appreciated the difficulties the Clerk had had to face and agreed with his ruling, this having been done out of tender consideration for the feelings and judgement of minorities or those who might be supposed to be so.

The Epistle was then read, approved and signed. Yearly Meeting was over.

But the debate was not. As the editorial in the *British Friend* in July said, it was not surprising that the dogmatic rejection by a few Friends of the terms Fatherhood of God and Brotherhood of Man and what they implied should not only have startled the whole Yearly Meeting but sent a thrill of sorrow and pain to many hearts, the effect of which a number of Friends found it difficult to cast off. Letters poured in to *The Friend* and *The British Friend* for months, some simple and forthright, some erudite and exegetical. Howard Nicholson wrote apologising for all the pain and sorrow he had caused and for his lack of Christian courtesy; he did not hold a limited, Calvinistic view of the atonement; he was merely afraid of universalism (John 1.72, R.V.). Rufus Jones stressed the twofold aspect of fatherhood and, like William C.Braithwaite and Edward Grubb, believed that while God was unquestionably the father of all, with the attitudes of a father, there was the further, realised or fulfilled relationship in which the likeness of children to their father was a possibility for all. Scholarly articles continued to appear in the *Friends Quarterly Examiner* and *Present Day Papers* but gradually the storm subsided with only an occasional late rumble.

Shock though it was to many Friends and surprising though it may seem to many today—as indeed is the absence of any reference to what early Friends had said about the bond between all who followed the Light as vouchsafed to them—there were circumstances which make the debate more understandable. There were Friends who held Adventist attitudes not unconnected with their peace testimony; war to them could never be abolished in the hearts of men until the coming of the Prince of Peace. The past, moreover, was still present. Though liberal theology was beginning to prevail in the Society, there were still those who clung to the doctrine of the atonement, the spiritual descendants of those responsible for the anguish of David Duncan and the early loneliness of Edward Grubb, and English as well as Irish evangelicals who, despite their smooth blanket phraseology, made a clear distinction between the sons of a creator and the sons of a redeemer. There was still suspicion of emphasis on the living awareness of the Inward Light made by those who linked it with the Fatherhood of God and Brotherhood of Man. Looking back at the history of the Society from its first revolt against creeds and dogmas, this debate can be seen as one further step in freeing the truth of God in human experience from all the church had done to embellish and condition it just as French collectors once decorated the exquisite, classic simplicity of Chinese porcelain vases with ormolu.

The question of religion and politics, closely connected with different concepts of God, has long been a matter of contention, from Amos to David Jenkins. At the turn of the century there were Friends who tried to suppress the application of their principles to international issues and to whom the Fatherhood of God and its corollary, the Brotherhood of Man, must have smacked of doctrinaire socialism. The Boer War presented Friends with a new kind of challenge to their peace testimony. They did for the most part recoil from exuberance in victory and the more vulgar excesses of the war spirit—the blow your nose for Britain campaign would not have encouraged many Quakers to buy its special handkerchiefs—but there were eloquent apologists for Government policy even in aspects difficult to reconcile with Quakerism and who could still stereotype the Calvinistic, God-fearing Boer as a despicably cruel and corrupt foe. With few exceptions these were Friends who were also defending the evangelical tradition they held so dear.

There had been mounting tension within the Society for some time before Yearly Meeting, open disgust over the re-hash of the fifty-year-old Crimean Peace Appeal and growing exasperation with both the Peace Committee and especially Meeting for Sufferings for what seemed a feeble response to need for action. John Morland, who was so fair as Clerk to Howard Nicholson during Yearly Meeting (fair to a fault, many thought), had said there had been a distinct impression of slackness. Arguments continued throughout the war over an extraordinary range of topics—the wording of the eighth Query (our twenty-first) about war, the sending of milk to babies in concentration camps, the glorification of Lord Roberts, who was said to have prayed for his men with tears in his eyes. Friends were themselves casualties of the war, wounded as well as vulnerable, hurting each other in their own hurt, but somehow, even during Yearly Meeting 1900, preserving something that enabled the Society to survive and learn and grow. Even at their most contentious, perhaps they saw each other as more than proclaimers of acceptable or unacceptable convictions and, like themselves, as children of a God who was more than the subject of their debate.

In 1977, when I had to reflect aloud on the Yearly Meeting just concluded, I began by saying I would have found it easier to reflect on the London Yearly Meeting of 1900. Edward Milligan agreed with me afterwards about the need for historical perspective in reflection. I am glad to have been able to attempt it after all and in this way, for him. I only wish I could have found and produced the text of that paragraph excised from the draft Peace Address. God alone knows what was in it; but then, he was there.

THOMAS RICKMAN
IN
FRANCE

by Alex Kerr

The Quaker architect Thomas Rickman (1776-1841) is recognised as a significant figure in the Gothic Revival of the early nineteenth century. If his designs for churches and other buildings have not met with unqualified praise from later critics, he is nonetheless remembered as an indefatigable antiquarian of early architecture, whose textbook, which first appeared in 1817, remained a standard work throughout the nineteenth century. In this book, *An Attempt to Discriminate the Styles of English Architecture from the Conquest to the Reformation*, Rickman was the first to propose the set of terms, now so familiar, for the different styles and periods of architecture in the Middle Ages: Saxon; Norman; Early English; Decorated; Perpendicular.[1]

In his early years Thomas Rickman had followed various occupations, in pharmacy and medicine, in a corn-factor's business and an insurance company, but in 1817 he finally set himself up in an architect's practice, turning what had been his hobby into a profession, and one which he followed with some considerable success and recognition for the rest of his life.[2] He travelled frequently about Britain making detailed notes and drawings of ecclesiastical and other ancient buildings, the fruits of this research appearing in successive and enlarged editions of the *Attempt*. Four editions appeared in his lifetime and three more were brought out after his death by the publisher and antiquarian John Henry Parker.

Thomas Rickman travelled abroad only twice, on each occasion making a brief visit to Northern France. (A sketch-map showing the route of each tour appears overleaf.) These journeys are adequately documented, since

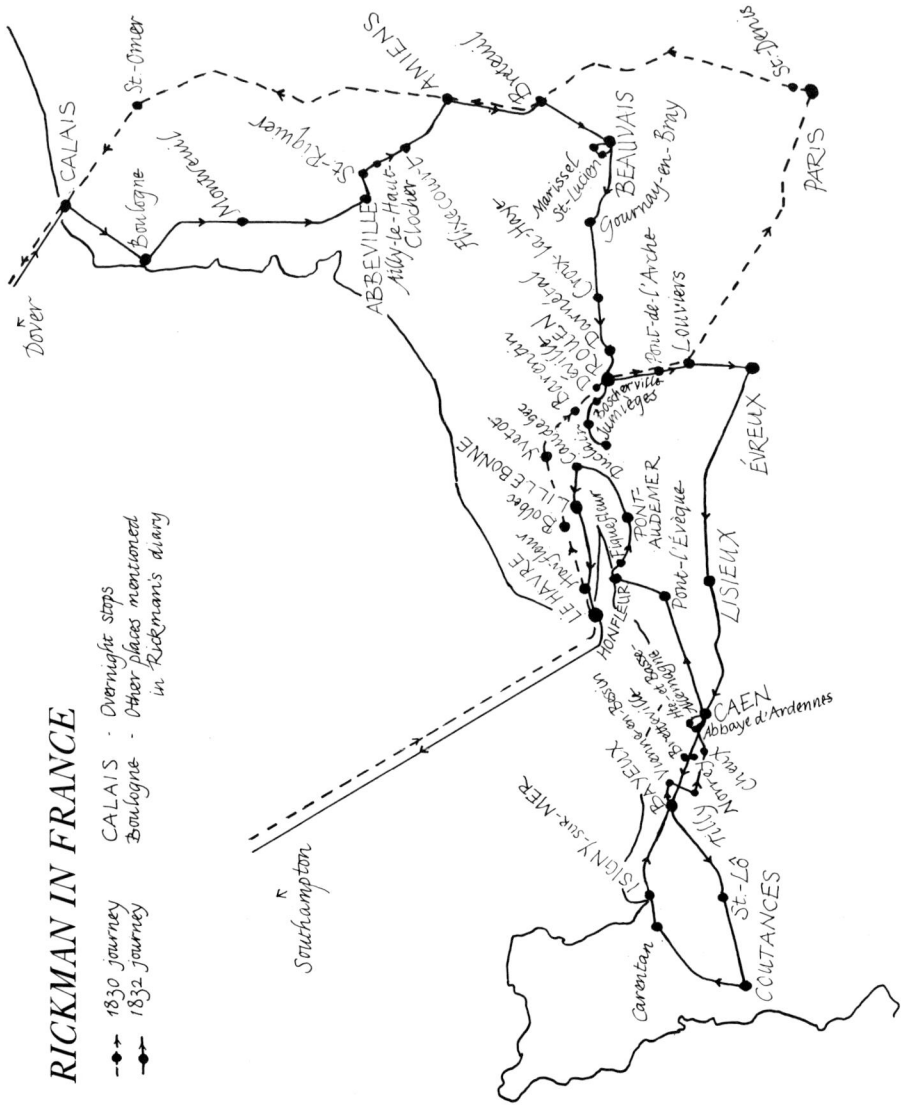

RICKMAN IN FRANCE

1830 journey   CALAIS - Overnight stops
1832 journey   Boulogne - Other places mentioned
                         in Rickman's diary

Rickman kept a diary, begun in 1807 and maintained until he was over-come by ill-health in 1834. At the period of his life with which we are concerned, a page is devoted to each day, with the date at the top and a note of the day's weather at the bottom. Every few days he also jotted down his out-of-pocket expenses.[3]

In May 1830, in the company of his partner and former pupil, Henry Hutchinson, he made a hurried visit to Paris, travelling out by way of Southampton, Le Havre and Rouen. From the diary it sounds as if Rickman went more as a tourist than as an antiquarian architect pursuing serious research. It is true that in Rouen he examined various well known medieval churches, but he did not make detailed drawings until his second visit two years later. Here is his diary entry for the day he spent in the city:

> 1 5 23 [Sunday, May 23rd]
> I was up early this Morning & went up to St. Catherine's. The finest City view I ever saw; the absence of smoke made everything so clear. St. Ouen rises most magnificently & is a finer church than any I have seen. During the day I visited many other Churches. I saw most of the Streets in the City, many very old & very narrow, but the necessity of going off to Paris tomorrow rendered it impossible to note anything. I went over the River into St. Sever before dinner, to which Jones from Havre [a Canadian whom Rickman and Hutchin-son had met at their hotel on landing in France] joined us & we tried to go up Mathurine but a heavy storm came on so that we gave it up & had some fine lights on St. Ouen. We went with Jones to a Caffe to eat Ice.
> bright—warm—Stormy

The next day Rickman notes that on the journey from Rouen to Paris they 'passed among many fine Churches of good decorated work which are undrawn and seem unknown', but strangely enough, during his three days in Paris, he makes no mention of visiting any medieval ecclesiastical buildings, but rather lists such landmarks as the Louvre and Luxembourg Gardens and the Jardin des Plantes, the northern boulevards, the Inval-ides, the Ecole Militaire, the Père-Lachaise cemetery and the windmills of Montmartre. A letter had been awaiting his arrival in Paris informing him of an appointment back in Birmingham to discuss work on Lord Bradford's country seat, Weston Hall, and this necessitated his early return. He set off on 27 May and travelled apparently non-stop for three days, by way of Calais, Dover and London, until he reached home.

From the diary one may deduce that no stop was made at Saint-Denis (indeed in mentioning the place Rickman seems more concerned to record his boyish delight at the fact that the *diligence* in which he was a passenger overtook one carrying an earlier travelling-companion), and yet there is a drawing of the abbey church in the collection of Rickman's drawings from his French journeys, now in the Bodleian Library in Oxford (MS dep. b. 140). The original of this may, however, itself have been copied by Rickman from some other architectural drawing.

This first, truncated visit to France appears to have left little impression on Rickman's serious antiquarian work. The second journey, which he undertook in 1832 is more significant.

We should perhaps pause to notice that this was a period of change in Rickman's life. Since 1827, he and Hutchinson had been occupied with designing and supervising the building of New Court and the 'Bridge of Sighs' at St John's College, Cambridge. Rickman was making a number of valued new acquaintances in university and scholarly antiquarian circles, and it was at this time that he met William Whewell, Fellow (later Master) of Trinity College, Cambridge, with whom he was to make his tour of Picardy and Normandy. In January 1830 Rickman was informed of his election as a Fellow of the Society of Antiquaries and in June New Court was opened.

Before the visit to Paris in May 1830, Henry Hutchinson suffered a bout of ill-health. During the following year he steadily declined and in November 1831 he died. Richard Charles Hussey worked in his place on several projects with Rickman at this time and in 1835 became a partner in the architect's practice.

Although his life within the Society of Friends had not been without times of difficulty, Rickman remained faithful in attendance at meeting for worship at least until the early 1830s, often recording in his diary his reflections on the spoken ministry. In 1804 he declared his intention of marrying his cousin Lucy Rickman, but as Friends disapproved of the marriage of first-cousins, the ceremony was performed before a priest of the Church of England, and they were disowned. When in 1813, after several years as a widower, Rickman wished to marry Christiana Horner he applied to be readmitted to the Society and was accepted. In 1812 his meeting, Hardshaw, at the request of his old monthly meeting, Lewes & Chichester, called him to account for his absorbing interest in medieval ecclesiastical architecture and for the close links he had formed with the established church now that he had secured contracts for new church buildings. Friends were satisfied, however, when he assured them that his work 'might be hereafter a pecuniary benefit'! In 1832 Rickman and his third wife, Elizabeth Miller, whom he had married in 1825, first attended Edward Irving's church in London, a connection which became ever closer in later years. At the end of his life Rickman left the Society of Friends and was received into Irving's Catholic Apostolic Church.

William Whewell had travelled through Northern France with the writer and antiquarian Kenelm Digby in 1823 and had visited the Low Countries and Germany in 1829, examining medieval architecture and publishing his findings in his *Architectural Notes on German Churches* in 1832. On 7 August in the same year Whewell and Rickman set off together from London and crossed from Dover to Calais to start their tour. This time Rickman kept more careful notes and drawings of the buildings visited and sent back four letters to the President of the Society of Antiquaries, which were later read to meetings of the Society in London. They were subsequently published in the Society's journal, *Archaeologia* (vols. 25 (1834) and 26 (1836)). Substantially the same material appeared in the fourth edition of the *Attempt*, published in 1835.

Rickman, as usual, kept a careful record of his expenses along the way. We find, for example, at the head of the page in the diary for 7 August 1832 this little account:

coach	1. 10. –
Book	–. 3. 6
London	1. 12. –
Cant[erbur]y	1. 15. –
to Dover	–. 5. 6
Passage	11. 6
	5. 17. 6

Their tour took them to many of the major churches and cathedrals in Picardy and Normandy as well as a number of interesting smaller parish churches and other ancient buildings. Rickman records that over one hundred buildings were examined.

After looking at Boulogne and Abbeville, Whewell and Rickman visited Saint-Riquier. Rickman believed that the church there seemed to have escaped the notice of French architectural antiquarians and he was pleased to note features which supported his theory that closer parallels could be drawn between developments in English and French medieval architecture than most scholars, particularly those on the Continent, had accepted:

5 8 9 [Thursday, August 9th]
We looked at some Churches in Abbeville and abt 10 set off by a Hackney Coach and 2 Horses for St. Riquer, where we found a most admirable church, perfect and unmutilated, & unwhitewashed & undescribed. It has parts of several Dates & is a most important link in our Chain of examination. We went across to Ailly-le-Haut-Clocher & examined several Churches. Dined at Flixcourt and got to

Amiens. Time enough to look into the Cathedral & to finish a letter home & write up my notes.

bright—hot/87—clear

After inspecting various churches in Amiens, they travelled on to Breteuil and Beauvais, where Rickman recorded:

> 7 8 11 [Saturday, August 11th]
> We have today very carefully examined the Cathedral & the Old building, the Ancient Cathedral, which proves to be very early, having Roman Bricks like Brixworth [in Northamptonshire] & resembling it in several respects . . .
> bright—Hot/82—cloudy

Rickman was fascinated to find several such parallels with pre-Conquest English architecture and made careful notes and drawings of this old part of Beauvais Cathedral, known as the 'Basse Oeuvre', and later of the Church of Saint Germain in Rouen, the walls of Bayeux, and the Roman theatre at Lillebonne, which he put to good comparative use in his paper entitled 'On Saxon Architecture' (*Attempt*, fourth ed., pp. 299-308, an emended version of the paper that was to appear in *Archaeologia*, vol. 26, pp. 26-46). He had mixed feelings about the extremely lofty Gothic main structure of Beauvais Cathedral, however. In a second paper, 'On the Architecture of a Part of France' (*Attempt*, fourth ed., pp. 309-21, and *Archaeologia*, vol. 25, pp. 159-87), he levels the general criticism at French medieval churches of 'a want of clearness of outline' and, as a prime example, cites Beauvais Cathedral, because 'having no nave, only choir and transepts, it looks at a distance a heavy lump and it is only when near enough to distinguish some of its admirable details, that it can be properly appreciated'. He expands on this when he writes of a feature common in French churches but rare in English ones, the termination of the east end 'in a circular or polygonal apsis; this with the chapels and aisle surrounding these apsis, lends very much (aided by the lofty and extensive flying buttresses) to give that lumpishness mentioned above' (p. 310).

The tour was not without inconveniences. For example, of the journey after Beauvais, Rickman wrote:

> 1 8 12 [Sunday, August 12th]
> . . . the Diligence was very slow and made many unnecessary stops so that we did not reach Rouen till past 5 [they had set off on the fifty-mile journey at 6 a.m.]. We breakfasted at Gournay, when a Gens d'Arme made a fuss abt the Passport but his officer passed it as all Right, and other Gens D'arme at Croix-de-la-Haye & Darnetal asked for it. This provisional Gens D'arme having probably little else

to do makes a fuss abt Passports while those in great towns hardly ever ask for them.

     bright—hot/81—clear

Later, after visiting Caen, Rickman and Whewell met with more suspicion:

> 4 8 22 [Wednesday, August 22nd]
> We set off abt 9 o'Clock & on the Road saw two fine Spires, one a little way out of the Road. We sent the Coach to Bretteville & went down to Norrey, when we had the Key brought & went into the Church. When we had been in some time, a body of people came and told us to go out, which we did, and drew outside, when up comes a Sargeant Major of the Nat. Guard and takes us to the Mayor's, & neither of them, Mayor or Adjoint, being in, he examined our papers, with which he was not satisfied, kept us prisoners $1\frac{1}{2}$ hours in the Mayor's house, then March'd us up to Brettville to the Mayor there with 2 N. Gds with fowling Pieces and 2 with Sabres. This Mayor was a Gent. who soon told the NG they had no business to disturb us & set us at liberty . . .

Whewell in a letter to his aunt, Mrs Lyon, written from Winchester on 2 September 1832, recounts this incident and adds: '. . . when Rickman produced his printed card, the Mayor of Bretteville sagaciously observed that "Monsieur n'aurait jamais *improvisé* un timbre comme celui-là," and moreover that it was very important to preserve a good understanding between France and England, and so dismissed us, much to the discontent of the National Guard of Norrey'.[4]

On their travels they met several illustrious French antiquarians, who welcomed them and accompanied them on visits to local sites of interest. At Rouen Augustin Le Prévost entertained them and conducted them to the abandoned and recently ruined abbey at Jumièges and later he went with them to Evreux, where he showed them round the cathedral and introduced them to the German architect Ramy and to the Prefect of the *département*. In Caen, and later at his home in Vienne-en-Bessin, they met the best known antiquarian of medieval French architecture at this time, Arcisse de Caumont, according to Rickman 'a most intelligent and indefatigable Man'. Rickman records: 'I gave him one of my books & found he had made great progress in a similar Classification of French works for the Society of Normandy' (Diary, 27 August 1832).

After Le Prévost left them at Evreux, Rickman and Whewell continued westwards to Lisieux and Caen and its surroundings. Rickman categorises several of the churches he saw according to the terminology he used for English buildings: Lisieux Cathedral—'a very fine Specimen coming nearer to our EE [Early English] work than any we had seen'; Basse Allemagne—'One of the best EE churches with some Norman work we have seen'; the Abbey of Ardennes—'the finest dec. [Decorated] church we have seen'.

They travelled on to Bayeux, Saint-Lô and Coutances, the most westerly point of the tour, before returning to Caen via Carenton and Isigny-sur-Mer. This part of the tour seems to have been more hurried and Rickman records little detail in his diary of what he saw, although he did make architectural sketches. He was particularly impressed by the church at Isigny, which he mentions as being a beautiful example of the Decorated style.

As 'On the Architecture of a Part of France' is an apology for the comparative method in architectural studies, Rickman is at pains to find parallels between English and French examples. It was therefore with relief, no doubt, that he discovered at least these few good examples of what he would like to term Early French and Decorated buildings, which he admits are much rarer than their English counterparts. He does not accept the classification proposed by Caumont but believes that his own divisions for English styles may be applied to French ones. However, he does state: 'the last period, . . . being in its arrangements so peculiar and so different from our Perpendicular style as to require a different appellation, I take the name given to it by Monsieur de Caumont, and which is particularly applicable, . . . Flamboyant' (*Attempt*, fourth ed., pp. 314-15).

As they turned eastwards to make for Le Havre, the weather broke and it was cold and showery for their visits to Pont-l'Evèque and Honfleur. Strong winds in the Seine Estuary prevented the steam-boat ferry crossing between Honfleur and Le Havre, and so they travelled round by Pont-Audemer, Caudebec and Lillebonne, which gave Rickman an opportunity to examine a number of 'curious' churches and the Roman theatre. On 31 August they boarded the *Camilla* for Southampton at the end of their twenty-five-day sojourn on French soil.

Rickman's childlike general enthusiasm shows through in his diary, but it is characteristic of him that in 'On the Architecture of a Part of France' he should dwell on small details he had observed, so that he felt obliged several times to compare French buildings unfavourably with English ones. He draws attention to what he saw as very inferior church towers with pack-saddle roofs—an 'unsightly mode'—and poorly designed parapets—'there are still very many village churches with dripping eaves'. We must remember, however, that many ancient ecclesiastical buildings in France were in an even more ruinous state than those in England at this date; well-informed restoration was still in its infancy on that side of the Channel. Rickman returned home with renewed conviction about the value of comparative study. (If he had been able to travel a little farther south, he might have had greater difficulty in relating the churches there so closely to his own system.) His commitment to the comparative method is clearly stated in the closing sentences of the essay where he writes that we should:

> ... study the styles of architecture in different countries, not as contradictions, but as members of the same family with local differences.
>
> If this is done with a basis of extensive English knowledge (for I think that in England will be found the most clearly marked features of each style in its purity) then will every succeeding essay, giving details of buildings in any part of Europe, be eminently useful, and lead the way to what is much wanted—a general statement of the progress of architecture in Europe; and why may this not hereafter enable us to acquire some systematic knowledge of the Moham-medan and Hindoo buildings, to which we are but strangers at present.
>
> (*Attempt*, fourth ed., p. 321)

It was left to Rickman's successors, the Parkers and the Banister Fletchers, to follow this comparative method through.

Whewell gave his own account of their journey in an appendix to the second edition of his book on German churches.[5] The high regard which he had for Rickman is expressed in the preface of the third edition, published after the architect's death, where he describes his outstanding contribution to the study of medieval architecture and calls him 'that excellent and sagacious man' (p. xiv). He and Rickman remained firm friends in the years following the tour of Northern France. They corresponded about competitions for buildings in Cambridge (in which Rickman was unsuccessful) and sent one another reports of medieval buildings they had examined. Whewell sent letters with marginal sketches to Rickman on his returning from a tour of Scotland in 1834[6] and after a visit to Ireland in 1835.[7]

To conclude, here is a charming and affectionate glimpse of Rickman on his French tour seen through Whewell's eyes. In a letter sent from Caen to his sister Ann he describes the wonderful, traditional muslin and lace headdresses of the women in the Normandy countryside and writes:

> ... We admire them as we meet them in the street, and the admiration is generally mutual, for my companion is also a remarkable figure in his way. He wears the Quaker dress, which of itself would draw

some notice here, and being a little, round, fat man, with short, thick legs, and a large head, he sets off the dress to great advantage.

It is a difficulty for me to saunter along as slowly as he walks, and as, besides, he is perpetually running from one side of the street to the other to peep into whatever catches his attention, our motions are very irregular and apparently ill connected; and we seldom move far without the honour of some special spectators.

Notwithstanding this I like my companion very much. He is very good-humoured, and very intelligent and active, and I see more by travelling with him than I should do alone, besides understanding the architecture much better.[8]

NOTES

[1] Rickman actually published the first version of his essay in James Smith's *Panorama of Science and Art* (Liverpool, 1815). See Nikolaus Pevsner, *Some Architectural Writers of the Nineteenth Century* (Oxford, 1972), chapter v, 'Rickman and the Commissioners', pp. 28-35.

[2] See Thomas Miller Rickman (Rickman's son), *Notes on the Life and on the Several Imprints of the Work of Thomas Rickman, F.S.A, Architect* (London, 1901), and John Leslie Baily, 'Thomas Rickman, Architect and Quaker: the Early Years to 1818' (unpublished Ph.D. thesis, Dept of Fine Art, University of Leeds, June 1977).

[3] Rickman's diary comprises fifty-seven pocket books, bound in red leather, each measuring $6\frac{1}{2}'' \times 2\frac{3}{4}''$ (16.5cm×7cm). They are now in the library of the Royal Institute of British Architects, London. Where I have quoted from the diary I have generally left Rickman's spelling and use of capital letters unchanged, but I have emended or added to his erratic, largely absent punctuation.

[4] Quoted in Mrs Stair Douglas (Whewell's niece), *The Life and Selections from the Correspondence of William Whewell, D.D.* (London, 1881), p. 147.

[5] 'Notes Written during an Architectural Tour in Picardy and Normandy', in *Architectural Notes on German Churches* (Cambridge, 1835), pp. 129-235. Reprinted in the third edition (Cambridge, 1842), pp. 227-333.

[6] Quoted in Isaac Todhunter, *William Whewell, D.D.* (London, 1876), vol. II, pp. 190-92.

[7] A copy of this letter, dated 31 August 1835, is in the library of Trinity College, Cambridge (MS 0. 15. 46 (45)).

[8] Quoted by Mrs Stair Douglas, pp. 145-46.

THE ESSENCE OF FRIENDS HOUSE: A VIEW FROM THE CENTRE

by Jon North

Those who live away from London after working at Friends House for a long time look back from the real centre of the Society, the local meeting, with a mixture of nostalgia and incredulity. The incredulity must be similar to the visitor's who asks, entering the massive portico in the monumental façade on a typical working day, 'What is there to see here?' There is little in this 'Quaker centre' to detain a sightseer: a cathedral, or a stately home, has much more to offer. Friends House is a shell for contents less easily assimilated by a casual visitor. So the building which was part of my working life for over ten years seems curiously remote from the distance of a country meeting in the Midlands.

The nostalgia relates almost exclusively to people, those who were colleagues and became friends. Many of them were not Quakers, which made their devotion to our quirks and practices the more touching. Devotion is not too strong a word for the effort and care that goes into the work at all levels. There is room, too, for the nostalgia of pride in solid achievements left behind. Those who administer library and archives, and who plan building alterations, tend to leave behind tangible results more readily than most, and it is a satisfying thing to do.

Friends House has a number of different images to its different users. The vast majority of these are outsiders, visitors who enter on business which has only secondary reference to Quakerism. They may be commercial representatives intent on making a sale; or visitors to the Library for research into family history; Book Centre customers; maintenance engineers; or most likely some of the many thousands who attend meetings at Friends House in rooms hired for the purpose. Whatever the building is to them, it is almost certainly not a focus for religious witness or social and international action.

To many others the building is simply a shell in which their particular occupation is located for the time being. Late at night it is once again deserted and silent, left to the wardens in their eyrie and the occasional vagrant who has eluded the final security checks. Almost everyone who uses Friends House has a lopsided view of this shell which is labelled Quaker.

One of the problems is that it is hardly labelled. There are signs and notices—more now than there were. But somehow in the massive stone surroundings of the exterior and the public areas inside, the notices are hardly seen. And they are functional rather than declamatory. Many meeting houses, in their smaller-scale settings, manage better to announce the presence of Quakers than does Friends House in Euston Road. This is partly a hangover from Quaker plainness, which is only very slowly being eroded by revolutionary suggestions about media, advertising and so on. The reticence arises partly from another Quaker problem: that we don't quite know, nowadays, *what* we are trying to advertise, and when people hit on a formula it often seems to tell only half a story. But at Friends House I think it also comes from the fact that it is not true to say (as one would at a local meeting house): 'Here are Quakers'. There are some, and there's a good deal of paper explaining about Quaker this and that, but as a whole the occupants are not identifiably Quaker.

I am not trying to run down the staff. It is a dedicated group. Nor is there the same worry about Quaker identity as the Friends' Schools continually face with few Quaker pupils and fewer staff. There is a fair number of Friends working at Friends House, and those in key positions are able to interpret the Quaker message well. However, the uneasy relationship between a massive office block full of non-Quaker events twelve hours a day or more and the Sunday meeting for worship which draws its members from a wide commuter radius is a slightly uneasy and lopsided one. Unlike a local meeting house, whose focus is the membership in worship, Friends House is in danger of lacking a soul, and so it fails to proclaim itself decisively. Even those staff who wish to worship daily sometimes express guilt at 'wasting time' attending the fifteen-minute meeting held each morning!

This difference between Friends House and a local meeting house is reflected in lettings policy. Friends House has an 'open door' policy which would hardly suit most local meetings. To the Euston Road administration lettings are mainly a means of making money for the Yearly Meeting Fund and so easing the burden on hard-pressed local contributors. The social service is there of course—groups without any other home often find a meeting place at Friends House and so defuse what might otherwise become confrontations or more violent outbursts. So is the familiar conflict between the uses the Society wishes to promote—often at short notice— and the longer-term planning of outside groups' events. But in local communities such as those served by most meeting houses, the identity of the Society is such that it likes to restrict the use of meeting houses to loosely 'like-minded' groups. Preference for social usefulness also prompts local Friends to offer comparatively low rents which often barely cover running costs. A meeting house can easily be a community centre as perhaps all local churches should be. Friends House is very far from that.

The images of 'the London office' range from the crowded to the echoingly empty, from the noise and bustle of Yearly Meeting or a large conference to the night gloom lit only by the orange glow of street lamps. Quaker escapologists know, almost blindfold, the back ways and second exits from the building, used by staff on occasion to avoid a persistent enquirer. For most visitors Friends House is a maze, of which one pathway is known—the route to a meeting or office—while the others are similar and perplexing ways to confusion. There are huge spaces encasing pipes, girders or rooftops in the generous architectural 'backstairs' style of the 1920s. And there are the stores and archives which contain both the fruits of past witness and the seeds of future Quaker truth, in the shape of paper of all kinds. Administrators of premises and of archives have care for the opposite ends of this 'paper chain' which passes by or through almost every other department of the Society's work in the process of transformation. We Friends are incorrigible paper-pushers.

This is an essay based on affection. I do not propose sweeping changes or radical alternatives. For one thing, the main value of the building is in its position. It is at a good point on the national road and rail networks for a Society vitally dependent on communication, including human contact from all quarters. Business video links are well in their place, but worship through an electronic network is not very successful, as Yearly Meeting overflows and broadcast meetings have often shown. For another thing, feasibility studies of different arrangements are technical as well as human studies of very great complexity. Above all we need to take stock of what we have, and not always be proposing exciting changes. Reformers should remember that if we cut costs by reducing paid staff, we are likely to increase the demand of the part-time voluntary substitutes for practical back-up services. In that case Friends might be in danger of employing people only to do humdrum jobs they themselves had not time or skill for, while the creative developments were undertaken by committees which come and go. At that point the Friends House office would lose its heart. Its strength is in commitment to the needs as well as in the skills required to satisfy them, and there is already a tendency for routine work to overwhelm some offices so that creative development is difficult to fit in.

I look back from my small meeting, and I do feel remote from the physical surroundings of Euston Road. But it is a comfortable remoteness, because I know that there are plenty who work at Friends House who are exemplary trustees of our work and witness, and because to me, like many others, actually being in central London is a necessary evil rather than an enjoyable experience. There are few who work at Friends House who can feel fully involved in their local meetings while they spend their working hours immersed in Quaker business, so withdrawal presents the chance of strengthening local fellowship. I can find time for the local meetings and their small concerns with renewed energy. The caution of the 'civil servant' can be abandoned. The fresh air of the countryside will benefit my soul as well as my lungs.

WOMEN IN THE
SOCIETY OF FRIENDS

by Janet Scott

Independence of men and humble dependence on God has ever been a characteristic feature of the service of a woman Friend.
Friends Quarterly Examiner, 1879, p. 460

The Society of Friends has always declared the equality of women with men. The way in which it has practised this equality has often been influenced by the attitudes of society and culture outside. Yet in the Society of Friends theology is often formed by practice. It could be said that we do it first and think about it afterwards! Therefore, to discover what the Society believes means scrutinising both what is asserted and what is done.

This essay looks at some aspects of the history of women in the Society of Friends, relating it particularly to the development of theology. It concludes by raising some questions for this century. The information which is here was gathered with the help of Edward Milligan and his staff. I am glad to have this opportunity of expressing my gratitude, not only for Ted's help but for his friendship.

Women played their part in all aspects of the Society's life in the early stages so that they contributed to the formulation of both practice and theory. The Society's understanding of itself was slow to develop, but Fox came to see it as 'a gospel fellowship, a gospel order, a holy community and a fellowship of evangelism'. That is, it was a community called out and led by Christ, who was himself the priest and teacher of his people; it was so ordered that the will of God was known; the members cared for each other, both physically and spiritually, so that holy lives were led; the truth was to be preached throughout creation. The experience on which this was based was one where women were seen to be active as preachers and evangelists, in the visiting of prisoners and care for the poor, and in which women as well as men suffered persecution.

There were fourteen women amongst the Valiant Sixty. One of these was Elizabeth Hooton, the first convert to Quakerism. She was involved in the spreading of the new movement and by 1655 had been imprisoned four times. She travelled twice to Massachusetts where she was flogged, and she died whilst accompanying Fox on a mission to Jamaica in 1671/2.

Another was Mary Fisher, imprisoned in York, whipped in Cambridge, examined for witchcraft in Boston; though best known for visiting the Sultan of Turkey (1660), she also travelled to Barbados and the West Indies. Henry Fell wrote from Barbados: 'Mary Fisher is a very pretious heart and hath been very servicable here'. She met her first husband, William Bayley, when she was visiting prisoners in Newgate. He described her as 'a woman with the face of an angel'.

Less well known to us amongst the early women arc Katherine Evans and Sarah Chevers, who faced the inquisition on Malta and who, when compelled to attend Mass, turned their backs on the altar and prayed loudly; and Elizabeth Fletcher, who was only about fourteen when she was brutally beaten in Oxford, who preached in Ireland and died, in 1658, at the age of nineteen or twenty.

London women Friends were particularly well organised and active. They included Anne Downer, one of the leading women preachers. In 1656, Fox, in prison in Cornwall, sent for her to prepare his meals and act as his amanuensis. Then aged thirty, she walked to Launceston from London. She probably wrote down one of Fox's most famous epistles (*Journal*, p. 263), the one which includes 'Then you will come to walk cheerfully over the world, answering that of God in every one'. It is interesting to note that in some other epistles Fox refers to that of God in every man, and fascinating to consider whether Anne Downer was responsible for the, to us, more inclusive usage. The friendship between Fox and Anne Downer was such that in 1686, when she was dying, Fox made a special journey to be with her.

Anne Downer became treasurer of the Box Meeting. This began in about 1659/60 when Sarah Blackbury (in whose arms Richard Hubberthorne died in Newgate) took to Fox a concern about the poor. She and Fox gathered sixty London women Friends at short notice and set up the meeting, of women only, to relieve necessity among Friends. The Box Meeting still exists today.

Another leading Friend was Rebecca Travers. She was convinced by James Nayler, and though she was not involved in the events which led to his condemnation, she remembered her early debt by washing his wounds after he had been scourged. For some time the Morning Meeting met in her house.

At Swarthmoor Hall too there was organisation in support of Friends; financial support, hospitality and letters of comfort and guidance were supplied. Margaret Fell, in particular, took political action, making direct approaches at different times to both Cromwell and the King.

Women were also active in writing tracts and testimonies. Margaret Fell was probably the first woman to write a theological tract justifying the place of women. It was called *Women's Speaking justified . . . etc* and was published in 1666 when the author was in prison in Lancaster. Her argument is a piece of skilful and original biblical exegesis, drawing on many texts from both testaments. She points out, for example, that in Genesis 1, 27, male and female are created equally in the image of God. She then goes on to argue that, since in Genesis enmity is declared between the seed of the woman and the seed of the serpent, those who speak against the woman and her seed's speaking speak out of the enmity of the old serpent's seed. She points out too that women were sent with the news of the Resurrection. 'Mark this, you who despise and oppose the message of the Lord God that he sends by women: what had become of the redemption . . . if they had not believed the message that the Lord Jesus sent by these women?' She deals with the real problem passage in Paul's letter to the Corinthians (1 Corinthians 14, 35-36) by pointing out that it was written to a disorderly church. The women there were still under the law, not under the spirit.

This brings us to the basic theological justification for the equality of women and men in the Society, the idea that Christ restored all things to where they were before the Fall. As Fox wrote in his journal (p. 667): 'Man and Woman were meet-helps before they fell and the image of God and holiness and righteousness; and so they are to be again in the restoration by Christ Jesus'. This restoration justified not only equality in the Society, but the form of gospel-order which involved separate women's meetings, and the view of marriage as being between equal help-meets. Hand in hand with the equality of women in the church is the equality of the partners in marriage, both putting God's work first. Fox saw his marriage with Margaret Fell in 1669 in these terms, and as a symbol of the future rule of God. It was a symbol of the church come out of the wilderness and its marriage to the Lamb. In Epistle 264 he wrote: 'The Marriage of the Lamb is come . . . and the everlasting gospel order shall be preached again as it was among the apostles; and the gospel order shall be set up . . .' Both church-order and marriage-order then rest on an inaugurated eschatology, that it is possible here and now to live under the reign of God.

From 1666 Fox was setting up this gospel-order, the monthly and quarterly meetings, and the women's meetings. The process took some time and resulted in a mixed pattern. For example, in London, because women's meetings already existed, no separate monthly meetings were set up.

There was some controversy over the separate meetings for women and they provided one of the issues in the Wilkinson-Storey controversy. They were attacked on two fronts, firstly that men should conduct the business, secondly that men and women should meet together. It was easier to meet the first argument than the second.

The matter of women's meetings is considered in a number of Fox's epistles. That women should conduct business is argued in 308, 'That all that had received the gospel might be the possessors of it', and in 248, 'that none may stand idle out of the vineyard'. Fox held that all should practise their religion and be serviceable; less flatteringly, he thought that idle women would talk and tattle and judge with evil thoughts. For separate meetings he added biblical exegesis (Ep. 320) showing how the women met in the Old Testament, and more practically, argued that there were some matters which could not be spoken of before the men. Fox laid on the women's meetings particular practical tasks: the training up of young women, both in religion and in education and apprenticeship; the care of the poor, of children, and of servants; and the regulation of marriages. It is interesting to note, however, that his own marriage does not appear to have gone before the women's meeting.

It is difficult for us to see any reason for the separate meetings, but we may see some of the effects. They showed that women had their own authority and did not need the presence of men to legitimate their business. They encouraged women to practise public speaking and the conduct of business. They built up the expectation that Quaker girls would be useful—and this was reinforced by the Society's concern for education for girls as well as boys.

Strangely, no women's yearly meeting was set up in Britain by Fox, though women in Ireland and America had their own yearly meetings quite early. However, women were part of the ministers' gathering at YM, and the London women's meetings appear to have answered the epistles from women's YMs overseas. There was certainly a meeting of women Friends at the time of YM long before a women's YM was set up.

It is interesting to note the involvement of American Friends in the history of London YM. There was a great deal of interaction by letter and by travel in the ministry. In 1784, Rebecca Jones was one of the visitors. Her name is noted among the thirty-seven women and fifty-nine men ministers present. It is recorded in the *Memorials of Rebecca Jones* that she was part of the deputation from the women to the men, asking for the women's yearly meeting to be established:

> One Friend expressed the sentiment that it would be preposterous to have a body with two heads, to which R.J. responded that there was but one *head to the body which is the church*, and that in Christ Jesus male and female are one. (p. 65)

The women not only showed their superior grasp of theology, they won their point, and the YM was established as a meeting for discipline.

The women's YM actually appears to have developed another informal, but very necessary function, that of ensuring that young unmarried men and women Friends met each other. Though the prospect of disownment for children who married out is never mentioned in this connection, the women's YM seems to have taken the responsibility for arranging religious meetings for the young people who were present at YM. Marriages may have been made in heaven, but mothers helped them along.

In the nineteenth century, as Friends emerged from the Quietist period, the Society reflected some of the inequalities of society at large. However, the powers open to women Friends were large compared to women's restricted role in other religious bodies. They had freedom to preach and pray in public, and to hold offices in the Society. The recorded ministers in particular had a high public status; and this was the formal backing which the Society gave to Elizabeth Fry.

Quaker women had the contacts and the experience to organise for philanthropy. In the United States, Lucretia Mott was active in the anti-slavery movement. It was when she came to Britain as a delegate to the 1840 Anti-Slavery Convention, only to be refused recognition because she was a woman, that she gained the insight, impetus and contacts which became the springboard of the women's movement in the United States. Though Lucretia Mott was introduced to Elizabeth Fry, the latter was very cool towards her, for Lucretia Mott was a Hicksite Friend and not recognised by London Yearly Meeting.

With the impetus of the women's movement in the United States and the growth of higher education for women the system of separate business meetings began to crumble. Writing in the *Friends Quarterly Examiner* of 1879 on a visit to Western YMs, Richard Littleboy reported that, 'Joint sessions of men and women Friends are frequently held, our sisters occupying in all the Western YMs a position which is not assigned to them in England. All important Committees consist of both sexes, and in Indiana Yearly Meeting, while the discipline was in course of revision, women Friends were expected to take a full share of the work'.

One of the precipitating factors in the discussion of joint YM sessions in London was that of the American correspondence, when only one letter arrived from a joint YM instead of two, one for men, one for women. Who was to answer it?

The problem surfaced in 1894. By this time, many MMs and QMs had begun to meet in joint session at least part of the time. Both the Home and Foreign Mission Committees were mixed, but Meeting for Sufferings was all male.

In 1894-95 the question of a joint YM was discussed throughout the Society. The 1895 YM set up a joint committee to report the following year. In the meantime the Manchester conference was held. A new spirit of liberal theology was moving in the Society. In 1896, after much discussion, the Yearly Meeting accepted the principle that women Friends form a constituent part of all meetings for church affairs equally with their brethren. From that point, change was rapid. Though practical difficulties meant that women were not able to be appointed to Meeting for Sufferings until 1898, within ten years of the decision separate business meetings for women had ended.

What is interesting to note, however, is the type of argument that was used in discussing the issue. Typical is the editorial in *The Friend*, April 1895, which points out practical issues: if women sit with men they must forego the valuable women's meetings; there is no meeting house large enough for the joint Yearly Meeting; when men and women meet together, men monopolise the time.

In the discussion in YM 1896, as reported in *The Friend* the arguments put forward are often practical, or, if they deal with principle, for the most part they refer to concepts such as justice, equality, and responsibility. Only one Friend, Joshua Rowntree, is recorded as referring to biblical sources ('There is neither Jew nor Greek, bond nor free, male nor female in Christ Jesus') or to the principles on which the Society was founded and structured. Much more common are arguments expressed in liberal and humanist terms. As William Edward Turner said, 'We could not in the Society of Friends resist the spirit of evolution and progress now working amongst us'.

As we look back over these episodes, perhaps we now have to ask whether the 'spirit of evolution and progress' is sufficient. Fox grounded the equality of women in the Society on a distinct interpretation of Christian theology based on biblical exegesis, and on a church order and a concept of marriage linked to the demands of the rule of God. Has the Society of Friends in the twentieth century lost this theological understanding? If it has, is our understanding of the equality of women based on the sand of progress or on the rock of the Holy Spirit?

BIBLIOGRAPHY

George Fox, *Epistles* (London, 1698).
Margaret Fell, *Women's Speaking Justified, Proved and Allowed of by the Scriptures, etc.*, (London, 1666).
Hugh Barbour (ed.), *Early Quaker Writings* (Grand Rapids, 1973).
M.R.Brailsford, *Quaker Women* (London, 1915).
W.C.Braithwaite, *The Second Period of Quakerism*, second edition (York, 1979).
J.L.Nickalls (ed.), *The Journal of George Fox* (London, 1975).
Isabel Ross, *Margaret Fell, Mother of Quakerism*, second edition, edited by Edward H.Milligan and Malcolm J.Thomas (York, 1984).
Elfrida Vipont, *George Fox and the Valiant Sixty* (London, 1975).
I.L.Edwards, 'The Women Friends of London', *Journal of the Friends Historical Society*, 47, 1 (1955), pp. 3-21.
R.Littleboy, 'Notes of a Visit to the Yearly Meetings of Friends in Western America', *Friends Quarterly Examiners*, 13 (1879), pp. 276-92.
The Friend (1894-96), *passim*.
F.B.Tolles (ed.), *Slavery and 'the Woman Question'. Lucretia Mott's Diary, 1840*, Friends Historical Society, Supplement 23 (London, 1952).
W.J.Allinson, *Memorials of Rebecca Jones* (London, 1849).

THE COMMITTEE ON GENERAL MEETINGS 1875-83

by Malcolm J. Thomas

When *The Friend* warmly greeted the 1881 Home Mission Conference (organised by the Friends First-day School Association, an independent body) and the appointment by London YM in the following year of a Home Mission Committee, it looked back at the steps leading up to them. These it saw as the formation of the FFDSA in 1847, and of the Bedford Institute (from 1865 the Bedford Institute First-day School & Home Mission) in 1849; and the minute of London Yearly Meeting 1875 which encouraged the holding of general meetings and appointed a committee to that end.[1]

In 1868 London YM had received a report from a committee of its Yearly Meeting of Ministers & Elders which wondered whether it was

> worthy of serious consideration whether the time is not approaching for a revival in some places of those General Meetings embracing wider areas, which were so extensively held during the last century . . .

Little seems to have been done as a result: the general meetings which were to be a feature of Quakerism in America and the United Kingdom for some twenty years stemmed rather from Indiana YM's initiative in 1867, when it first arranged them 'for teaching, for discussion of central truths and practices, and for outreaching evangelistic work' (as Rufus Jones summarised it in *The Later Periods of Quakerism*). Other 'Gurneyite' yearly meetings (New York for example in 1871 and New England in 1872) followed; their epistles to London and to Ireland YMs often referred to their holding and their success; reports of them were carried in the British and American Quaker press—usually favourable ones in *The Christian Worker* (Chicago), *Friends' Review* (Philadelphia) and *The Friend* and *The Monthly Record* (London) and more critical in *The Friend* (Philadelphia) and *The British Friend* (Glasgow).

At their Yearly Meeting in 1874 Irish Friends appointed a committee to consider 'General Meetings as held in the bounds of most of the yearly meetings in America . . . and with liberty to hold such'. The first, at Grange, in Ulster, and the surrounding area, attracted nearly 5,000 people to some twenty-five meetings held over a week in June 1874. London YM, held a fortnight after Ireland's, had considered whether to recommend general meetings to its quarterly meetings, on receiving the epistle from Ireland. A number of Friends (Isaac Brown, Thomas Barrow and Jonathan Grubb among them) spoke forcefully in their favour. J.B.Braithwaite cautiously 'hoped that in the various quarterly meetings we should feel whether it would not be our place to enter into exercise as to the propriety of holding such meetings', while William Ball thought the matter might be left to quarterly meetings, which were at liberty to hold them anyway. William Graham (inevitably) opposed them and Charles Elcock dissented from 'the encouragement held forth' in Ireland YM's epistle: 'Irish Friends were sufficiently lively of themselves'. It was not until the following year that the committee (initially of twenty-three Friends and for a year) was appointed 'to assist Committees which Quarterly Meetings may appoint, to carry out the service, where openings arise, under the guidance of the Heavenly Shepherd, of such General Meetings'.

The appointment was not unresisted. A yearly meeting committee charged to see if it was needed favoured general meetings in principle, but some of its members clearly wondered, like William Ball, whether the matter could not be left to quarterly meetings. Conservative Friends again spoke against the whole idea, connecting it (like Joseph Armfield) with the visit of the American evangelists Moody and Sankey and 'the exalted religious feeling that during the last few months has pervaded the land'. *The British Friend* of June 1875, although believing there was 'an opening for service in this direction' and that the decision was 'a judicious one, and, it is to be hoped will answer its design—the institution of a more *aggressive* policy', recognised the uneasiness of some Friends by printing in its August number a letter from 'X'. This cited observations

> in some of the public papers, that the wave of Revivalism has at length reached the Society of Friends; a religious body thought to possess such elements of stability as to shield it from the danger of being drawn within its vortex,

and attacked, quoting *The Times*, methods which tended 'to encourage, in a great many cases, an unreal and sensational form of religion—a religion which mistakes physical excitement for spiritual change'. The same number prominently featured William Pollard's article 'The Present Crisis in the Society of Friends', which had already appeared in the July *Friends Quarterly Examiner*. He feared that the Yearly Meeting had acted with 'precipitancy . . . apparently in imitation of the doings in Ireland and America . . . before half the Society in England fully realise what is meant by a General Meeting'.

Jonathan Grubb (to be perhaps the most active attender, with Henry S.Newman, of general meetings throughout the country, as well as travelling widely in the ministry as an individual) had argued in *The British Friend* of February 1875 that George Fox and early Friends had adapted themselves to the needs of 'the people at large' by 'thrashing meetings' (a term used in America for Friends' revival meetings), distinct from 'retired meetings' or meetings for worship for Friends, which were inappropriate for the general public. An editorial of comparable length rejected his views. Friends who had already resisted the reading of the Bible in meetings for worship, and singing in Friends mission meetings (a list of nearly forty was published by Theodore Fry of Darlington in 1875) and First-day schools, saw general meetings as a further evangelical threat to Friends' principle of silent waiting in worship. The example given by the American minister Allen Jay during the discussion in London YM 1875, of a quarterly meeting which had grown from 800 to 4,000 members because that quarterly meeting had 'moved forward in faith' also raised fears of an influx of members brought into the Society through revival meetings and hence unaware of 'Friends' distinguishing principles'. *The Friend* of September 1875 was firm in its view that new members might result from holding general meetings, but that this was not a primary object; it stressed, however, that the

> services of a General Meeting are well fitted for calling into exercise a variety of spiritual gifts and of consecrated talent. There is a place for the preacher, a place for the administrator in arranging times and places for meetings, a place for those who teach rather than preach, in private conversation with inquirers . . .

The suggestion of new orders in the church equally struck a warning note for conservative Friends, especially after the American separations in Iowa YM and Western YM in 1877 and Kansas YM in 1879, seen as the result of aggressive revivalism and, in the case of Western YM, specifically over the appointment of a committee on general meetings. They should, however, have derived some comfort from the composition of the committee. Despite William Tallack's characteristically testy suggestion that 'any dozen Friends of average intelligence and earnestness would do perfectly well', the twenty-three (with three added in 1878 and another two in 1879) formed a weighty body.[2] Almost all were frequent speakers at yearly meeting; of the twenty-eight, eighteen were ministers when appointed and six more became ministers after; over half had travelled overseas in the ministry; most were involved with First-day schools; over a third were to be members of the Home Mission Committee. The committee had a firm base of moderate evangelicals, and even the most evangelical acknowledged Quaker limits.

The central committee's first task was clearly to get in touch with quarterly meetings: responses varied. London & Middlesex appointed its committee of twelve men Friends (including three central committee members, George Gillett, Henry Binns and Stafford Allen). Western QM's committee included two central committee members (George Phillips and Henry S. Newman). Suffolk QM quickly organised a general meeting at Bury St. Edmunds for July 1875. Bedfordshire QM, having asked its monthly meetings to consider the subject, concluded in October 1875 that they were 'unprepared to nominate Friends to take part . . . yet feel great interest in the subject'; in response to renewed urging it appointed a committee of twenty-two men and women in 1876. Durham QM (with no member on the central committee) had its own committee from October 1875. The committees of Western QM and of Sussex, Surrey & Hants QM distributed almost identical statements (possibly originating in the central committee) in August and September 1875, to enlighten Friends:

> By a General Meeting we understand a series of meetings held in the same locality, with the object of spreading the knowledge of Jesus Christ and His gospel, bringing souls to Him, and building up His people. The main purpose is therefore the same designed in our ordinary 'Public' Meetings [which were claimed to be] . . . too fugitive in their character to produce much permanent result. The holding of General Meetings is not the commencement of any new institution, but the revival of an old custom within our Society. Such meetings were frequently held by early Friends . . . but with the decline of ministry . . . they were generally abandoned, though Armscot and Brigflats meetings have survived as relics . . .[3]

At Yearly Meeting in 1876 the central committee was able to report that general meetings had been held at Bury St. Edmunds, Calne, Thirsk, Plymouth, London, Bridgwater, Newport (IoW), Gloucester, Leeds and Newcastle upon Tyne, and that all but one had been attended by members of the committee. Meetings had also been held at Lothersdale, Bentham, Settle, Otley and Gildersome (by Yorkshire QM), at Lynn (by Norfolk QM) and at Swarthmoor (by Westmorland QM); all these had been carried out under the auspices of the local QM committee, although members of the central committee had been present at some. The report went on:

> The interest awakened among Friends generally in efforts of this kind, has appeared to require but little, if any, stimulus from the Central Committee. It has been found best to leave the arrangement for each meeting to the Committee of the Quarterly Meeting... But... we have been able to assist the Local Committees by... writing to Friends of other parts of the country...
>
> As the main purpose of General Meetings has been understood to be that of preaching the glad tidings of a Saviour's love, the chief interest has generally centred in the meetings for worship and the mission meetings. A meeting for worship has generally been held in some central point, every evening... of the General Meeting, which has been from three to eight days; in addition to which, mission halls and chapels in surrounding localities have been occupied simultaneously wherever opportunities offered. In some places gatherings in the open air have been held... Other meetings have been held of a more special character. In some places the children have been assembled; on other occasions the young women, the young men, and the mothers...
>
> [As to] its influence on our own Society... At the first of these meetings, those who were engaged in promoting the object felt drawn previously to entering upon the service, to unite together to search the Scriptures, and for waiting upon the Lord... Similar opportunities have been arranged for at every succeeding General Meeting...

There was no essential change in this form during the lifetime of the committee: a general meeting held from 12 to 20 November 1881 at Gloucester was reported in *The Friend* of January 1882. It was attended by some eighteen Friends from other places, and commenced with a joint devotional meeting for Friends and workers from various mission halls placed at their disposal. On Sunday 13 November, thirteen meetings (and some afternoon Bible classes) took place at seven places in the town, with a total attendance of about 2,350 people; evening meetings were held at all seven locations through the week, as well as prayer-meetings each day, Bible-reading meetings, and special meetings for men, women, young people, mothers and teachers.

At Yearly Meeting 1877 the committee reported sixteen general meetings, most of them locally arranged; it hoped they might be more widely held, all having been within the same quarterly meetings as the preceding year. From 1878 it was able to state consistently that all meetings (over a dozen in that year) had originated in local concern. In 1882, when some fifteen were reported, 'the Committee has had very little to do with the arrangements in any direction, although at all times ready to render help . . . [since] Friends in their own localities have felt it laid upon them to carry out the work themselves'.

The need for work to be locally based had been plain even before the committee's appointment. William Ball at London YM 1874 had declared that a general meeting 'should of course be detached from invitation from without, or imitation even of our dear American Friends, and should arise from the true religious concern of the quarterly meeting'. The need for sustained concern, both at quarterly and monthly meeting level, became increasingly apparent. In 1877 the committee had noted 'new responsibilities, in the case of the General Meeting at St Ives, [Huntingdonshire,] which has been the means of gathering a considerable attendance in a place where there is at present no meeting of Friends, thus throwing upon Friends residing elsewhere [in the district] a deep responsibility'. It noted, too, an increased attendance at Leiston, Suffolk. In 1878 it recommended that the meetings be held in localities 'where the fruit may be watched over and harvested when the series of special meetings is concluded', citing St Ives, Leiston and Newport (IoW) as places where 'much good fruit remains' and an added responsibility lay on quarterly and monthly meetings. The following year

> ample testimony [was] brought before us that numbers of people have been truly converted to Christ through this instrumentality . . . In several cases, however, through there being no provision for shepherding the flock, many have joined other denominations; but we fear that many have also gone back into the world that might have been preserved . . . [T]here appears to be a serious need for the sustained efforts of Friends.

In the committee's report to Yearly Meeting 1880, its experience was summed up: the greatest success was based on existing mission work; the work had to be made permanent, not spasmodic, and not left in the hands of monthly or quarterly meetings which lacked the capacity to build on it; large centres of population where Friends had influence were promising areas; and, again, that general meetings should originate not with the central committee 'but in the lively concern of Friends themselves for the welfare of their own neighbours'. At the same Yearly Meeting, Western

QM sent forward a report from Hereford & Radnor Monthly Meeting, which stated that forty persons had been received into membership by convincement in the previous year (thirty-seven of them at Pales). Henry Stanley Newman

> said he was acquainted with all the 37 new members . . . They had not been received in bulk, but dealt with separately . . . This had not been any sudden movement—there had been for many years a leaning towards Friends; the work had been gradually growing up, and the General Meeting brought it to a point.

Jonathan Grubb thought this encouraging, 'especially in districts which were formerly populated by Friends. Ulster and the Dales of Yorkshire are such districts.' He also asked why Friends did not succeed in keeping those drawn to them by general meetings. In 1881 the central committee offered no report to Yearly Meeting, but during a session on small meetings Henry S. Newman recollected an old man at Pales General Meeting in 1879 who had spoken of having been reached by the Spirit and continued:

> I am reminded of the ostrich, who lays her eggs in the desert and watches them not . . . Do not, like the ostrich, go away and leave us alone, but do be content to follow up the work.

At Pales the work was kept up, largely by the new members themselves, but in other areas where no Friend was settled and no substantial body of new members received, it remained at risk.

In 1882 the committee rejoiced in the progress made. Acknowledging that

> other means and other modes of operation may meet the needs of the people more effectively in some districts, and the occasional holding of a General Meeting can never take the place of systematic home mission work or First-day School teaching

it regretted the many districts in which no general meetings had been held.

At each yearly meeting the committee's report came in for much criticism, largely on the grounds of singing, of co-operation with ministers of other denominations, and of the pre-arrangement of ministry. This did, however, give members of it an opportunity to clear themselves as individuals, implicitly indicting local Friends (or other members of the committee). In 1876 Francis Frith spoke for meetings held 'after the old-fashioned plan' as not only right but expedient (in that they offered something different) and against 'congregational singing'; Stafford Allen supported him. At Yearly Meeting 1877, Francis Frith went so far as to state his belief that 'the holding of general meetings will come to be, as it certainly ought, the principal means of reaching the public' but feared that it was 'a great mistake to suppose that we attract [people] . . . by leaving our old lines'. Henry S.Newman inquired what these old lines were:

> What we want is for all to look to the guidance of the Spirit. There are varieties of ministry. Some may be called to go out like George Fox did, and read and expound the Bible. Some individuals may be called, possibly, to sing a hymn. Some congregations even may be called upon to sing a hymn.

He again found support from Jonathan Grubb who claimed of the refusal to admit congregational singing, 'This is to me a one-man meeting!' Francis Frith had also seen (with perhaps these two Friends in mind) a tendency for general meetings to 'get into a particular groove. The same set of Friends attended them to some extent, some Friends having attended nearly all.' He had ceased to hold so cheerful a view by Yearly Meeting 1880, when he found some difficulty in replying to the conservative Richard Brockbank's question, 'whether the committee was at liberty to override the feelings of Friends living in those neighbourhoods where they held their General Meetings, and to introduce practices which have never been sanctioned by Yearly Meeting'. His answer, 'that the Friends on this committee did not feel bound to keep to any rule in regard to this matter in particular . . . The committee is not responsible for all that is done in them' can be taken with his later statement in the same session that 'the committee was not of much use' and that he (like Thomas Gates Darton) would be glad to be excused from it. William Pollard had regretted that 'we should have so many defects to consider in connection with this report every year' and other Friends expressed the wish that the committee should be made responsible for the conduct of general meetings or (failing that) be discharged. At the following Yearly Meeting Francis Frith thought the work done by the committee during the year had been very small. 'He was not sure whether it had been convened.' He had forgotten, or come to disagree with, J.B.Braithwaite's justification for the committee's existence in 1877:

> As to the committee there was so comparatively little active service, but yet he thought it might be well to have a committee as it just answers the object which Friends have in view, for whilst it does not interfere with the liberty of quarterly meetings, it might afford help where it was needed.

It was intended as, and remained, a facilitating, rather than an aggressive body, which was willing in 1882 for its work to be taken over by the newly-appointed Home Mission Committee (as it was when the Committee on

General Meetings was laid down at Yearly Meeting 1883): a recognition that the holding of general meetings could not stand alone and that the support needed to consolidate gains was more likely to be achieved by a body with more extensive aims and a solider base.

The appointment of the central committee had been a further move in the direction of corporate concern. J. B.Braithwaite had supported the initial appointment in 1875, contrasting 'services laid on individuals' and 'those which are laid on the church'. Francis Frith and Henry S.Newman had different views on the right holding of meetings, but were speaking the same language at Yearly Meeting 1877 when the one declared that 'it was in good ordering that a meeting should be held at the collective concern of the Church' and the other that 'these general meetings [arise] from the right concern of Monthly and Quarterly Meetings on behalf of the population that lies about them'. At Yearly Meeting 1882 Richard Brockbank had looked back over thirty years in which 'he had frequently heard that Church arrangements were to take the place of individual responsibility', when expressing his doubts over the Home Mission Committee. One of the participants in 'Jottings from a corresponding class', printed in *The Friend* of October 1882, might almost have been replying to him in writing that:

> The Friends of the 'middle ages' to a great extent did do without it [i.e. corporate action]. The reason they had no foreign nor home mission association was not altogether so much because they were selfish and lifeless, as because they thought every good word and work for the souls of men required *a separate individual call*. They could not understand a corporate call.

The committee's appointment had also been a recognition by the Yearly Meeting of one form of outreach and a means of bringing the question of mission work before Yearly Meeting. Its report of 1882 declared:

> Where General Meetings have been held and followed up, it has tended both to an increased spiritual life amongst our own members, as well as having been the means of winning souls to Christ from the masses of the population around.

Caleb R.Kemp, writing in his journal after attending Street General Meeting ('we held between 40 & 50 meetings altogether') in February 1881, thought it 'on the whole, the most satisfactory General Meeting that I have attended. Its influence, though, was more to lift up the Church in that place, than to bring in the outsiders who know not Christ'.[4] It was clear that the meetings had been one means of involving those vigorously evangelical younger Friends, already active in First-day school and mission activity, in officially approved work; and was thus a factor in strengthening those at the 1881 Home Mission Conference who wished to bring their work under the care of the Yearly Meeting, rather than establish it (like the Friends Foreign Mission Association) as an independent body.

General meetings were not, however, much longer to serve the purpose of the Home Mission Committee. It continued to support them where locally organised, from 1883 until 1886, when its report to Yearly Meeting noted that they had been replaced by 'series of meetings' (as they earlier had been in a number of American yearly meetings) of a less concentrated kind. Jonathan Grubb had foreshadowed the change in suggesting to Joshua Green in 1879 that

> In evangelistic meetings when we have a large mixed company too many ministers in a row does not answer well. All probably rightly exercised in spirit—but no room for the larger proportion of them.[5]

Henry S.Newman, addressing the Home Mission Committee annual meeting in 1886, concurred:

> Years ago there used to be a great waste of power in inviting ministers to a General Meeting, but they found by experience that they could do better by distributing themselves over a larger area. Therefore the plan in recent years has been to go on the apostolic plan of two and two . . .[6]

By this time there were six Friends who were workers in connection with the Home Mission Committee, settled at different places and supported or partially supported by the committee, and 'Friends in all parts of the country are watchful lest a separate class of supported ministers should be set up', as the committee's own report admitted: another fruit of 'revivalism' with American parallels which was to exercise non-evangelical Friends for some time to come.

NOTES

[1] The major sources for the work of this committee are printed either in the form of its reports (in London YM *Proceedings*) or in accounts of Yearly Meeting sessions and of many (but not all) general meetings in *The British Friend, The Friend* or *The Monthly Record*. No minutes, correspondence or other records of the central committee appear to have survived, although some records of quarterly meeting committees (in Durham and Yorkshire QMs at least) have. I have not been able to trace substantial bodies of relevant papers left by the most active members of the central committee.

[2] The membership of the committee was as follows: those in italics were recorded ministers at the time of appointment and those marked with an asterisk became so later.

1875   Stafford Allen (1806-89), London;
William Ball (1801-78), Tottenham and Kendal;
Henry Binns (1810-80), Croydon;
James Boorne (1824-1910), Reading;
Charles Lloyd Braithwaite (1811-93), Kendal;
Joseph Bevan Braithwaite (1818-1905), London;
Isaac Brown (1803-95), Kendal;
Thomas Gates Darton (1810-87), Peckham;
Francis Frith (1822-98), Reigate;
George Gillett (1837-93), London;
Joseph Jesper (1805-90), Preston;
Caleb Rickman Kemp (1836-1908), Lewes;
Richard Littleboy (1819-99), Newport Pagnell, Bucks;
Joseph James Neave (1836-1913), Leiston, Suffolk to 1876, then Australia;
Henry Stanley Newman (1837-1912), Leominster;
George Palmer (1818-97), Reading;
Thomas Pease (1816-84), Henbury, Glos;
George Phillips (1821-83), Milford Haven;
*Edwin Rayner Ransome (1823-1910), Wandsworth;
Isaac Robson (1800-85), Huddersfield;
*William Dillwyn Sims (1825-95), Ipswich;
*William White (1820-1900), Birmingham;
*Thomas Ashby Wood (1835-1914), Reigate to 1879, then Tunbridge Wells;
1878   *Alfred Tuke Alexander* (1842-1920), London;
*Thomas Barrow (1829-1919), Lancaster;
*John Fyfe Stewart (1845-1908), London;
1879   *Joshua Green* (1813-94), Stansted Mountfitchet, Essex;
Jonathan Grubb (1808-94), Sudbury, Suffolk.

³ London & Middlesex QM minutes, vol. 19 (1867-82), pp. 282, 291-92; *The British Friend*, vol. 33, 1.ix.1875, pp. 232-33; *The Friend*, vol. 15, ns, 3.vii.1875, p. 186; Bedfordshire QM minutes, vol. 1 (1865-82), pp. 128, 132, 140, 144. I am aware of only one work which has touched in any detail on the work of the central and local committees: in *Yorkshire Quarterly Meeting . . . 1665-1966* (Harrogate, 1979), pp. 304-07, W.Pearson Thistlethwaite skilfully disentangles an interrelated group of committees, including Yorkshire QM's committee on general meetings.

⁴ Journal of Caleb R.Kemp, vol. 4, 22.ii.1881, p.225 (Library of the Society of Friends, London, MS Vol S 6).

⁵ Jonathan Grubb to Joshua Green, 13.i.1879 (Library of the Society of Friends, London, Portfolio A/47).

⁶ *The Friend*, vol. 26, ns, 4.vi.1886, p. 169.

BIRTHRIGHT Y.Q., SEEKING CULTURAL
ANONYMITY BEHIND A PUNK MASK, IS FOILED
BY E.H.M.'S RESOURCEFUL MIND

by Leslie Webster

THE 1966 STATEMENT ON MEMBERSHIP IN THE RELIGIOUS SOCIETY OF FRIENDS: A MEMOIR

by Arthur J.White

The question of membership in the Religious Society of Friends is one that is always with us. There is a renewal of interest in the subject at the present time and if, as seems likely, London Yearly Meeting is about to face once again the revision of some of the basic material in its Book of Discipline, then questions affecting our understanding of membership are bound to arise.

There was a major discussion about membership in London Yearly Meeting in 1966. I remember it well. I had taken up the office of Recording Clerk on 1 May 1966, the seventeenth holder of the post since Ellis Hookes was appointed in 1657 at the age of twenty-seven years. I was somewhat older. On 27 May, I was sitting with the clerks, Godfrey C. Mace, Derek H.Crosfield and Dorothy H.Mounsey, at the table in the large meeting house at Friends House, London, at the opening session of Yearly Meeting, not knowing much of what I was supposed to do. I needed a guide, philosopher and friend, and he whom we honour in this book was available then and continually during my twelve years of service.

Yearly Meeting was involved in revising *Church Government*. During the whole of my service we were revising something or other and everyone else seemed to be doing the same. It was a time of change, in geographical boundaries, social and political organisation, groupings of various kinds, and in much fundamental thinking. London Yearly Meeting had completed its revision of *Christian Faith and Practice* in 1959. It was recognised that the work was incomplete without a revision of *Church Government*. Yearly Meeting in 1961 authorised such a revision and Meeting for Sufferings appointed a committee of twenty-five Friends. The Revision Committee held its first meeting, under the clerkship of Harold Reed, in September 1961, aiming to complete its work by 1964. It managed to complete the revision of the *Advices and Queries* by that date, Yearly Meeting approving the text at Newcastle-upon-Tyne. The whole of *Church Government* was finally approved at a Special Yearly Meeting in London in November 1967.

The revision process inevitably promotes the writing of reports, memoranda and preparatory documents and there are notable examples in Quaker history, but none more remarkable than the document *New Life from Old Roots: the Organisation of the Society of Friends*. This was made available to members of London Yearly Meeting as an interim report from the Church Government Revision Committee in preparation for a Special Yearly Meeting in November 1965. The report came to yearly meeting as the voice of the Revision Committee but the hand—who could mistake it?—was basically that of him to whom we are so indebted for the ability to 'set forth', if I may use one of his favourite phrases, the background material necessary for our forward thinking. I have wanted an opportunity to say this, for at a meeting of the Revision Committee (into whose councils I had been drawn during 1962 and had remained to be counted as a member), when the draft of *New Life from Old Roots* was presented, I had the foolish temerity to question whether its lively, flowing style, with touches of humour, felicitous quotations from the past so clearly pertinent to the present and with at times an abrupt directness, would appeal to Friends as they approached the task of revision in all its solemnity. Thank goodness nobody took any notice of me, for I have returned again and again to *New Life from Old Roots* with pleasure and much profit, and I am particularly thankful that the author took no umbrage.

New Life from Old Roots did not deal specifically with the question of membership though it made the comment 'that though it may be true that the Christian church is a divine-human society, it is no whit less a collection of men and women with all manner of human frailty—stupidity, pride, lust, ambition, jealousy'.[1] It also pointed out that membership in different organisations, like the National Trust or the Historical Association, varies. 'Membership in the Christian church involves loyalty to a person. It does not (or should not) therefore depend on sameness of interest or compatibility of temperament but must learn to thrive on a tremendous diversity of gifts, of needs, of outlook'.[2]

To return to the 1966 Yearly Meeting: on the Saturday morning Muriel

Poulter introduced a draft statement from the Revision Committee on membership and its meaning.[3] She referred to the ferment of thinking that was going on in the Society, as elsewhere, and to the diversity of opinions held about the nature of the Society and about membership. Some thought of the Society as a movement and felt that formal membership should be abolished; others that membership should be accorded on request to all who sought it; others that a credal emphasis should be introduced to ensure greater homogeneity; others that there was a place in the Society for all seekers after religious truth, wherever they were seeking it. The view of the Revision Committee, she said, was that membership should not be abolished but that the commitment and assumption of responsibility that membership demanded were essential to the Society's being an instrument in the working out of God's purpose for the world. If things seemed confused in the Society this was not because they had no adequate guidance about the nature of the Society but because they had not taken what they had seriously enough. In *Christian Faith and Practice* certain assumptions underlay the book as a whole; belief in God—not a God 'up there' but a God known inwardly, yet definitely more than a subjective psychological experience; belief that God was working out a purpose of love; belief that Jesus Christ was intimately, uniquely associated with the working out of this purpose. She went on to say that credal statements divided; the roots of living religion and of true unity lay at a deeper level—in the response that led to shared discipleship, to lives empowered by the same Spirit, bound to God and to other disciples by love.[4]

Muriel Poulter's introduction can still speak to us, but powerful as her words were, they did not lead Yearly Meeting to accept the draft statement on membership. I think it might be said that the written statement was not as broad in its understanding of the Society's condition as was Muriel Poulter's introduction. The opening paragraph of the statement said:

> As part of the Christian church the Society of Friends is, ideally, a community whose members are drawn into fellowship with God and with one another by their response to the living Christ. We seek together to follow him and to live in his power, that men may be brought to know God and that the divine love may find expression in all human relationships. Our human shortcomings result in continual failures in our discipleship. We are a company not of the righteous but of sinners seeking to grow into the fullness of Christ.

Despite a later disclaimer in the statement about the imposition of outward tests of belief and practice, it did seem to a number of Friends in Yearly Meeting to present a particular theological stance and the statement as a whole came under severe criticism. Yearly Meeting asked for a simpler statement, with 'words which will encourage and not deter the earnest seeker'.[5]

In passing, may I say that I cannot think that the phrase 'that *men* may be brought to know God' would find a place in a statement drafted by Quakers today, which indicates some advance in our sensitivity towards women over the last eighteen years.

Members of the Revision Committee met later on that Saturday of the 1966 Yearly Meeting to consider what to do. My contribution to the proceedings was to arrange a supply of sandwiches and coffee to keep them going. After much thought, the committee asked three of its number to revise the statement. These three planned such a revision over a meal at Schmidt's restaurant in Charlotte Street. It was not the first time that an informal committee had met in this restaurant (alas, it is no more) on the Society's business. There will be no record in Quaker history of the restaurants and railway stations and garden squares adjacent to Friends House where serious and perhaps far-reaching discussions affecting the Society's life have taken place. One of the three who met at Schmidt's was staying in Kennington over the time of Yearly Meeting and he was troubled at the thought that a mere revision of the statement would not meet the wishes of the meeting. He came to the view that a completely new draft would be needed. Late at night and in the early hours he walked the streets of London seeking the right words. He does not remember the route he took but does recall passing Lambeth Palace on two or three occasions. It did not occur to him to knock up the Archbishop of Canterbury, Michael Ramsey, to seek advice, though we may be sure that a conversation between them would have been edifying.

When the Revision Committee met—I think it was on the Monday at lunch-time—it had three drafts before it, two revisions of the original statement and the new piece of writing. The committee opted for the new writing and it was presented to Yearly Meeting on the Tuesday evening. Introduced by Marjorie H.Lee, it was, after a deep exercise, accepted with minor alterations. It forms the introduction to chapter 23 of *Church Government* and begins:

> 'George Fox and his early followers', wrote Rufus Jones, 'went forth with unbounded faith and enthusiasm to discover in all lands those who were true fellow-members with them in this great household of God, and who were the hidden seed of God.' Our Society thus arose from a series of mutual discoveries of men and women who found that they were making the same spiritual pilgrimage. This is still our experience today. Even at times of great difference of opinion, we

have known a sense of living unity, because we have recognised one another as followers of Jesus. We are at different stages along the way. We use different language to speak of him and to express our discipleship. The insistent questioning of the seeker, the fire of the rebel, the reflective contribution of the more cautious thinker—all have a place amongst us . . .'[6]

This statement on membership is a notable one. It was composed out of the spiritual struggle which I witnessed at my first Yearly Meeting as Recording Clerk. It reflects the way in which our decision-making processes can operate and the devotion of members of committees who give much of their time and their deep concern to the well-being of the Society. It reflects, in particular, the sensitivity and ability of the one who composed it, whose written contributions in the last three decades have been beyond valuation and to whom London Yearly Meeting of the Religious Society of Friends is, indeed, greatly indebted.

NOTES

[1] *New Life from Old Roots: the Organisation of the Society of Friends*, being Documents in Advance for Special Yearly Meeting, 5-7 November 1965, para. 14.
[2] *Ibid.*, para. 16.
[3] Yearly Meeting Proceedings 1966, pp. 7-8.
[4] See report in *The Friend*, 10 June 1966, pp. 670-71.
[5] Yearly Meeting Proceedings 1966, minute 19, p. 239.
[6] *Church Government*, London Yearly Meeting of the Religious Society of Friends (1968, 1980), section 831.

'WE SHALL NEVER THRIVE UPON IGNORANCE' (J.J.GURNEY): THE SERVICE OF JOHN WILHELM ROWNTREE 1893-1905

by Roger C. Wilson

From about the 1830s the Society of Friends was penetrated from the top by a new strain of Quaker evangelicalism. Its most active proponents were preoccupied with personal salvation, for others as well as for themselves. During the previous hundred years of the Quietist period there had been an excessive lack of ministry, and this had become characteristic of the unconsecrated silence of a great many of the meetings throughout the country. The evangelical strain provided a vigorous flow of ministry drawn from the Bible, often as if it were a reservoir of infallible texts. What both strains inhibited was reflective thought as of service to spiritual life. Yet for fifty years evangelistic ministry dominated the proceedings of London Yearly Meeting.

In the late 1880s and early 1890s, however, there was a growing revolt from below by hitherto frustrated Friends who effectively eroded the prolonged dominance of the evangelical strain, diminishing, but by no means overwhelming, its influence. This third strain longed that the Society should be emancipated from the thought-starved formalism of two hundreds years but had, at first, no coherent views of what they were looking for or of how to set about finding out. But arising out of the restlessness in the Society, Yearly Meeting in 1894 established a large

Home Mission Committee of about eighty members with an open remit to consider extension or outreach in any appropriate form. Its membership was nominated by quarterly meetings, thus covering a wide spectrum of Quaker outlook, including that of a small number of able, mostly young, members whom I think of as 'emancipators'. It also included a considerable number of experienced, evangelically minded Friends who were strongly committed to the continued prosecution of local evangelistic mission activity, in the hands of modestly paid 'workers'.

Astonishingly, within a year of its first working meeting the small group of emancipators induced the large, bemused Committee (which had forthwith undertaken to sustain the paid mission work) to forward a minute to Yearly Meeting proposing that a conference be held in Manchester in November 1895, to consider how the spiritual and historic heritage of the Society could be revitalised by facing the discoveries and perplexities of the real contemporary world with an enthusiastic Christian faith and ministry, reinforced by unfrightened entry into the limitless fields of mental and aesthetic experience.

From the point of view of the emancipators the Conference was a huge success. Over a thousand Friends spent three wintry days listening to, and to a limited extent discussing, more than thirty papers, most of them vigorously emancipatory in character. It was the first time that Friends had ever had the chance to assess the Society's position in the light of 'modern thought' and secular change, or to consider how the intellectual stirrings of its members could be related to their spiritual needs. But weighty conservative Friends were alarmed by the ferment, for the opening of the sluices had shown that there was indeed a widespread, eager hunger for what amounted to Quaker adult religious education.

Over the next dozen years this was met in a variety of ways—residential summer schools, the foundation of Woodbrooke, the appointment of qualified, itinerant educators, the inauguration of the Swarthmore Lectures and of Quaker historical scholarship.

What is immediately surprising is that, in face of the ferment emerging from the Conference, none of these developments owed anything to the official structure of the Society. Once the finances had been tidied up, the Conference simply disappears from the minutes of the Home Mission Committee. The clue to the explanation of what did not happen lies in the exchange of comments following papers in the Conference session on 'The Society of Friends and Modern Thought'. Papers had been presented by Thomas Hodgkin, John William Graham and Rendel Harris making the case for fearless study of the Bible, of Church and Quaker history, and the nature of religious experience. The paper by Sylvanus Thompson, a distinguished physicist and electrical engineer, had declared his sense of spiritual security in being at once a Christian, a Quaker, and a theoretical and experimental scientist. When the time came for discussion a Friend suggested that after these 'excellent papers no minutes' addresses would add to the strength of the meeting'. A large number of Friends concurred. Two weighty Friends of the evangelical strain accepted the proposal of no discussion 'on the understanding that many of us do not agree with many of the things that have been said'. A large number of Friends briefly concurred. Another Friend cried in anguish '. . . this Conference, representing London Yearly Meeting, cannot do justice to itself without placing on record a protest'. S.J.Capper: 'Many of us feel that never in our lives have we so appreciated the privilege of being Quakers as to-night'. There *was* no substantive discussion.

Nothing illustrates more simply the tension within the Society which stood in the way of any official action about whether or how to move towards educated religious freedom. This, of course, raises the question how the Friends of evangelical strain on the Committee and in Yearly Meeting itself had ever found themselves sharing responsibility for the organisation of a conference that turned out to be essentially radical. The answer lies in a fascinating study of diplomatic skill in the Quaker mode, but it is too long to develop here. That there *was* an effective outcome of the Conference was the result of unofficial private enterprise, at the base of which was the Christian passion, the intelligent imagination and the business entrepreneurial skill of John Wilhelm Rowntree.

For our purposes the story goes back to 1886 when trade was bad and the small Rowntree cocoa firm was struggling for life. Its head was Joseph Rowntree (1836-1924) whose character and work are delightfully presented by his grand-daughter-in-law, Anne Vernon, in *A Quaker Business Man* (York: Ebor Press, 1981). It was in 1886 that John Wilhelm left Bootham at seventeen to go straight into the factory, working through all the departments before taking charge of one of the units at the age of nineteen. He quickly showed innovatory management competence and at twenty-one was made a partner. Over the following seven years, Joseph's second son, Seebohm, and two of Joseph's nephews, Arnold and Frank, all joined the business in the same way and became partners at twenty-one. The firm recovered and prospered. The partners belonged to an extraordinarily able, intelligent family with quick, easy, enjoyable confidence in one another. They were united in seeking efficient growth of the business, incorporating responsibility to the employees as persons and to the customers for the quality of the product. To Joseph and his young partners the business, their Quakerism, their public interests and their private lives were all part of an integrated life-style, spiced with wit and full of ideas for doing better what needed to be done.

Throughout his life Joseph had a remarkable capacity for asking shrewd, critically constructive questions about everything in which he was interested—business, public life, the Society. Defined problems could be solved by rational, diplomatically conceived initiatives. In the cocoa works he drew in his young relatives as equals and lunch must have been the time for an enormous amount of analysis and talk with a view to action in all the matters in which they had a common interest. Perhaps it was because talk and mutual confidence was so easy that there is disappointingly little on paper about shared ideas and plans.

This was the setting in which John Wilhelm Rowntree grew to maturity. His boyhood had been difficult. Class work had been hampered by a hearing defect. There was a robust element of aggression and short-temper. But there was also wit and a passionate interest in amateur dramatics. In the earliest days of adulthood there was a period of spiritual despondency when he says that he would probably have left the Society if he had not been held as a birthright member in a strong Quaker family. As he found his emotional feet he made increasingly successful efforts to discipline his aggression though remaining sharp when occasion required. He was on good terms with the men on the works floor. At the age of twenty-six, when hearing was already getting harder, he had trouble with his eyes. He learnt from the consultant that he would probably be totally blind before middle age. Rufus Jones wrote later:

> Dazed and overwhelmed he staggered . . . into the street and stood there in silence. Suddenly he felt the love of God wrap him about as though a visible presence enfolded him, and a joy filled him, such as he had never felt before. From that time he was a gloriously happy man.

He continued to work at the factory until he was thirty. Then health compelled him to work from his home in Scalby. He died at the age of thirty-seven. Among the reflections made after his death Joshua Rowntree wrote in *The Friend*: 'As Francis of Assisi wedded poverty, John embraced physical infirmity. . . . He did not fret over his physical limitation; he treated it kindly'. In *The British Friend*, Edward Grubb wrote: 'Those who only saw his boyish fun [or] marvelled at his knowledge of art and stories which he poured forth from an apparently exhaustless store—scarcely guessed at what a white heat the passion for God and for man was burning below'. Or as Anne Vernon put it more coolly fifty years later: 'To be a man dedicated to God, and at the same time an asset in any social gathering, is an unusual combination'.

Now back to 1893. In that year the twenty-four-year-old John Wilhelm Rowntree startled Yearly Meeting on behalf of the hitherto silent young.

156

For years, he said, weighty Friends had gone on about the want of spiritual life among younger Friends. The fact was that Truth as presented from the ministers' galleries was simply incomprehensible, but the young did not find it welcome to say so to their revered elders. They felt so bound, hand and foot, by the conventions and language of the 'establishment' (not his word) that they could find no service in the meeting. What they needed was 'plain, uncontroversial sermons . . . upon the practicalities of life', and they must be in language that was understood. The meeting was electrified. William Charles Braithwaite, aged thirty-one, and Sylvanus Thompson, aged forty-two, spoke in support. J.Storrs Fry, for thirteen earlier years clerk of Yearly Meeting, spoke of his pained hope that the young would speak with ministers about their shortcomings. But this was not easily done. Later that year John Wilhelm wrote that it was no adequate answer to his generation to say that 'if they will be simple and lay aside their reasoning, they will soon find work in the mission field that will settle their doubts'.

The Society was shaken and the occasion was an uncomfortably persuasive contribution to the deliberations of the new 1894 Home Mission Committee when, early in 1895, it was persuaded to begin to plan the Manchester Conference. In the meantime there can be no doubt that the occasion and the reaction would have been carefully and constructively reviewed over lunchtime at the cocoa works. Neither Joseph nor John Wilhelm had been nominated by their quarterly meeting to the Committee, but two of their close relatives were—John Stephenson Rowntree, Joseph's grocer brother in York, and their rather younger cousin, Joshua Rowntree in Scarborough. Quaker life and service in all their aspects were continually matters for review within this intimate family circle and surely thought and plans mulled over at lunchtime in the works must have been passed to the group of emancipators on the Committee, whose influence increased when Joshua became chairman of its executive committee and of its conference sub-committee.

In the event, John Wilhelm contributed a paper early in the Conference on the theme 'Has Quakerism a Message in the World To-day?' and his father a paper in a later session devoted to 'The Effective Presentation of Spiritual Truth'. The core of John Wilhelm's paper is on page 82 of the Conference report: 'The Church exists to create for each succeeding generation the ideal of the Christ in the thought-form of the age, and in the adaptability of Christ's teaching lies one secret of its power'. This meant that Friends must take into their corporate religious life the vitality of contemporary biblical, scientific and social enquiry, together with the inspiration of refined aesthetic enjoyment, all held together in the well-known prayer with which he concluded his paper:

Then, O Christ, convince us by Thy Spirit, thrill us by Thy Divine passion, drown our selfishness in Thy invading love, lay on us the burden of the world's suffering, drive us forth with the apostolic fervour of the early Church! 'Speak to the children of Israel, that they go forward'.

Joseph's paper focussed on the need for prepared and educated Quaker minds and the consequent provision of a residential base which would equip eager young spirits 'for service in our meetings through the exercise of gifts of teaching or ministry', surely the germ of Woodbrooke. Most of the other papers were powerful presentations along converging lines towards emancipation so that the hitherto frustrated went home exhilarated and hungry, but the conservatives went away troubled.

After a year of Committee inaction John Wilhelm went into action. Early in 1897 he talked with George Cadbury about the possibility of running a small experimental summer school later that year. Letters in the Woodbrooke library show that by February he had talked it over with his Yorkshire relatives and it was possible to outline practical proposals, adding the hope that George Cadbury would help with finance—which he did. Detailed arrangements were quickly centered on York and in August the Summer School movement was effectively launched at Scarborough with some seven hundred Friends in residence for a fortnight's hard biblical, Quaker, and social study. John Wilhelm had originally intended to stay in the background since he thought of himself as still an *enfant terrible*. But Joshua proposed successfully that he should be pressed to serve as secretary from his desk at the Cocoa Works, writing that 'he [Joshua] finds JWR is now everywhere commanding confidence and respect in a way that 4 years ago he could not have said that he did'.

Over the next six years a Continuation Committee with Edward Grubb as secretary organised further schools at Birmingham (twice), Scarborough (again), and Windermere; by 1904 there was enough enthusiasm and local experience to develop summer schools in many parts of the country. The role of the schools was reviewed in the tenth annual report of the Continuation Committee:

> Scarborough in 1897 and Birmingham in 1899 were successful in arousing a considerable portion of the Society . . . to a sense of the need for Bible study in a spirit of loyalty at one to the facts of history and to the truth of Christian experience. Opposition was, indeed, encountered from many quarters—on the ground that the free handling of Scripture tended to undermine its authority, or that the human reason was placing itself where alone the Divine Spirit should be.

Two years earlier, the annual report had referred to John Wilhelm's death: '. . . his colleagues constantly leaned upon him for suggestions as to new lines of service and for wise counsel in times of difficulty'.

The summer school movement is the ancestor of every Quaker study circle to-day.

Papers in the Woodbrooke library show that, meanwhile, the shaping of Woodbrooke began at Yearly Meeting in 1901, when John Wilhelm spoke of his dream, again to George Cadbury, and drove home the point with the comment: 'I can see the walls of the college arising, built by GC'. In November of that year George Cadbury offered his home, Woodbrooke, as an experimental residential base for something to be done 'to remedy the lack of a thoroughly efficient ministry . . . in our meetings'. But he had no confidence in the central structure of the Society to run the experiment, which went ahead in the hands of George Cadbury, John Wilhelm Rowntree and a small group of Birmingham Friends.

Again plans matured quickly. In May 1902 it was John Wilhelm who wrote to Rufus Jones, asking him whether he would leave Haverford for two years in order to direct studies at the prospective Woodbrooke Settlement 'to train and equip . . . without exalting the intellect above the Spirit . . .'. Rufus had to decline and it was again John Wilhelm who, in December, went to Cambridge and successfully persuaded Rendel Harris to resign his fellowship at Clare in order to become the first director of studies at Woodbrooke in 1903.

At the same time as he was working on the start of these institutions John Wilhelm was laying the foundations of two other developments that have served Friends well ever since. One was the need for a new flow of written Quaker thought in contemporary language, of which there had been little for two hundred years except for the evangelical studies of J. J. Gurney. Towards this end John Wilhelm initiated and edited *Present Day Papers* from 1896 to 1903, picking up and developing themes opened up at the Manchester Conference. Some of the best of his own contributions are included in the posthumous memorial volume, *Essays and Addresses*, some of which are reprinted in *Claim Your Inheritance*, published forty years later by the Bannisdale Press. It is a pity that his essays lack the sparkle of his descriptive writing on his travels in Palestine and the West Indies.

The other writing of which he laid the foundations was the great historical study of the adventurous birth of Quakerism in the seventeenth century and of its subsequent vicissitudes. He was working on notes for this in the last years of his life.

In reflecting on and assessing the work of John Wilhelm Rowntree it seems to me that posterity has failed to recognise that he brought to it the disciplined use of time and energy which he had learned in the thirteen hard years between the ages of seventeen and thirty during which he was a senior business executive in a firm which was emerging from depression into rapid expansion. Even in retirement he remained a director and a few weeks before his death he presided at the company's annual meeting in the absence of his father. Part of his gifts were those of delegation and co-operation, working easily with very able colleagues and assistants. His ability to get things done, directly or indirectly, was thoroughly professional. Yet he never allowed professionalism, any more than intellect, to exalt itself above the Spirit.

Even so, the seeds that he had planted and nurtured with others might never have survived the lack of corporate financial support from within the official structure of the Society. It was the originally modest resources of the infant Joseph Rowntree Charitable Trust that made it possible to carry his initiatives into maturity. A sketch of the origins and early grants of this Trust appears in an article, 'Money and Power', in the *Friends Quarterly* of July 1972. Its first grant-making meeting was a month after John Wilhelm's death; its very first grant of £150 a year (shortly raised to £400) was made to Edward Grubb, 'realising the value of the services he might render . . . upon lines that would have commended themselves to JWR'. This was the beginning of an adequately qualified itinerant educational ministry in the Society in this century. Within the next two years the Trust shared with the Cadburys the expense of seeing Woodbrooke through its financial problems. It committed itself to the formal responsibility of financing the Quaker history over the next twenty years. In 1907 it initiated and financed to fruition the idea of the Swarthmore lectures, picking up John Wilhelm's concern for the regular publication of Quaker thought in printed form. And over the next twenty years the Trust carried the responsibility for sustaining and financing the great series of Quaker historical studies, the idea of which had been at the heart of JWR's work in the last years of his life.

It is appropriate to end this essay with two quotations. The first is from George Newman's 1905 obituary notice in *The Friend*: 'His sight almost gone, yet he saw more than others; his hearing defective, yet he heard what others fail to hear'.

The second is from John Wilhelm Rowntree's own editorial in *Present Day Papers*, September 1899: 'The mistake of most theological teaching lies in the fact that it is conceived as a crystal and not as a seed'.

A BIBLIOGRAPHY OF THE WRITINGS OF EDWARD H.MILLIGAN TO 1984

by David J. Hall and

Malcolm J. Thomas

If in relation to the learning of the author the number of his publications seems scanty, remember that (as he himself wrote of Henry J. Cadbury) he is 'generous to the point of profligacy in giving time to get the answers to other people's questions, or to read the drafts of their articles or books'. Whether as Eduard Milligan (Keith Robbins, *John Bright*, 1979), Theodore Milligan (Richard Fisher, *Joseph Lister 1827-1912*, 1977) or Edward Millikan (Harry Emerson Wildes, *Voice of the Lord*, 1965), his generosity has been widely acknowledged.

The compilers apologise if their oversight has reduced the bibliography further and wish that it had been possible and proper to identify all texts where Edward Milligan's hand has been at work. It has not been possible to include his writings in *The Star* (a duplicated house journal, 1941-1947, of Friends Relief Service); it should be noted, however, that articles appearing there under the signature 'Antiquax' (one of his later pseudonyms) were written not by Edward H.Milligan but by Lawrence Darton.

In all works listed below the place of publication is London, and the work in question is signed by the author, unless otherwise stated.

'The holding of YM' [a letter to the editor, signed 'EHM', Reading], *The Friend*, vol. 99, 3 January 1941, p. 12.

'Should all Friends keep hens? From a letter to the editor' [signed 'E'], *The Wayfarer*, vol. 22, March 1943, pp. 24-25.

'Friends and temperance' [a letter to the editor], *The Friend*, vol. 103, 7 December 1945, pp. 858, 860.

'Quaker service', *Friends Quarterly*, vol. 2, no. 2, April 1948, pp. 92-99.

Handbook for Friends [*on quarterly meeting procedure*, by Edward H.Milligan]. (Reading: Berkshire & Oxfordshire Quarterly Meeting, 1948, duplicated typescript.) [ii]+20pp.

'"Church affairs": some reflections on the seventh query', *The Friend*, vol. 107, 18 March 1949, pp. 209-10.

'Extension committees are still needed' [based on an address to Friends Home Service Committee], *The Wayfarer*, vol. 28, April 1949, pp. 59-60.

'Mere figures? A survey of the current tabular statement', *The Friend*, vol. 107, 15 July 1949, pp. 577-78.

'The ten duties' [to be reported by monthly to quarterly meetings], *The Friend*, vol. 108, 6 January 1950, pp. 11-12, with a correction, 13 January, p. 34.

'Final session of [London] YM' [letter to the editor], *The Friend*, vol. 108, 27 January 1950, p. 70.

Review of *Quaker Social History 1669-1738*, by W.Arnold Lloyd (1950), *The Friend*, vol. 108, 17 March 1950, pp. 198, 200.

Review of *Rude Forefathers: the Story of an English Village 1600-1666* by Francis Horner West (1949), *The Friend*, vol. 108, 12 May 1950, p. 352.

Review of *The Libraries of London*, edited by R.Irwin (1949), *The Librarian & Book World*, vol. 39, no. 8, August 1950, p. 124.

Review of *The First Minute Book of the Gainsborough Monthly Meeting of the Society of Friends 1669-1719: vol. 2, 1689-1709*, edited by Harold W.Brace (Lincoln, 1949), *The Friend*, vol. 108, 6 October 1950, p. 742.

'Membership and pastoral care. An address given to Sussex, Surrey & Hants QM held at Brighton on April 28th/29th, 1951', *Friends Quarterly*, vol. 5, no. 3, July 1951, pp. 143-58.

Review of *The Mysticism of Simone Weil*, by M.M.Davy (1951), *The Friend*, vol. 109, 31 August 1951, p. 772.

'Katharine Cumming Boswell' [(1889-1952: an obituary], *The Friend*, vol. 110, 17 October 1952, p. 917.

'Unequally yoked: a tabular survey', *The Wayfarer*, vol. 31, November 1952, pp. 169-71.

'The Darbys of Coalbrookdale' [review of *Dynasty of Ironfounders: the Darbys and Coalbrookdale*, by Arthur Raistrick (1953)], *The Friend*, vol. 111, 3 April 1953, p. 316.

Review of *Sudbury Quakers 1655-1953*, by Stanley H.G.Fitch (Sudbury, Suffolk, 1954), *Journal of Friends Historical Society*, vol. 46, no. 1, Spring 1954, pp. 38-39.

'Children's membership: a survey', in five parts, *The Friend*, vol. 112, 19 and 26 March and 2, 9 and 16 April 1954, pp. 243-45, 269-71, 295-97, 321-23, 343-45.

'About those dreary statistics' [the tabular statement], *The Wayfarer*, vol. 34, January 1955, pp. 6-7.

Review of *London to Philadelphia*, by Caroline C.Graveson (1954), *Journal of Friends Historical Society*, vol. 47, no. 1, Spring 1955, p. 47.

'A life of service' [review of *Arnold Rowntree—a life*, by Elfrida Vipont Foulds (1955)], *The Wayfarer*, vol. 35, February 1956, pp. 19-20.

'Philadelphia's "Faith and Practice"' [review of Philadelphia Yearly Meeting's book of discipline (Philadelphia, 1955)], *The Friend*, vol. 114, 3 August 1956, pp. 691-92.

'Beginning where we are' [review of *Prudence Crandall, Woman of Courage*, by Elizabeth Yates (New York, 1955)], *The Wayfarer*, vol. 36, February 1957, pp. 24-25.

'Children's membership', *The Wayfarer*, vol. 36, May 1957, pp. 67-68.

'The worshipping community and its meeting house. An address to the Friends' Home Service Committee on Sunday, April 7th, 1957', *Friends Quarterly*, vol. 11, no. 3, June 1957, pp. 98-109.

'A centenary' [Samuel Tuke (1784-1857) of York], *The Friend*, vol. 115, 18 October 1957, p. 931.

'A brace of clerks' [John Wilkinson (1783?-1846) and Samuel Tuke (1784-1857), clerks of London Yearly Meeting], *The Wayfarer*, vol. 36, December 1957, pp. 182-84.

'An unconventional Friend' [review of *Yardley Warner, the Freedman's Friend*, by Stafford Allen Warner (Didcot, Berks, 1957)], *The Wayfarer*, vol. 37, January 1958, pp. 12-13.

'Humility is endless' [Samuel Bownas' exercise as a minister], *Friends Journal* (Philadelphia), vol. 4, 8 March 1958, pp. 148-49.

'Statistics and the spirit' [a review of the tabular statement for 1957], *The Friend*, vol. 116, 2 May 1958, pp. 543-44.

'Event and meaning: reflections on "Documents in advance"' [signed 'T'], *The Friend*, vol. 116, 9 May 1958, pp. 572-74.

'Library exhibition' [on London Yearly Meeting since 1658, signed 'P'], *The Friend*, vol. 116, 13 June 1958, p. 767.

'Disciplined lives' [review of *Ernest E.Taylor—valiant for truth*, by J.Roland Whiting (1958)], *The Wayfarer*, vol. 37, July 1958, p. 110.

'Melchior and mistletoe: reflections on the Quaker celebration of Christmastide', *Friends Journal* (Philadelphia), vol. 4, 20 December 1958, pp. 743-44.

'Joseph Rowntree' [review of *A Quaker Business Man*, by Anne Vernon (1958)], *The Wayfarer*, vol. 38, January 1959, pp. 11-12.

'An outstanding American' [review of *Lucretia Mott—the Story of One of America's Greatest Women*, by Otelia Cromwell (Cambridge, Massachusetts, 1958)], *The Friend*, vol. 117, 27 March 1959, pp. 405-06.

'The life and times of Rufus Jones: Elizabeth Gray Vining's biography [*Friend of Life* (1959)] reviewed', *The Friend*, vol. 117, 29 May 1959, pp. 690-92.

'Library exhibition at Friends House' [signed 'P.P.'], *The Friend*, vol. 117, 21 August 1959, p. 928.

'An exhibition at [London] Yearly Meeting' [on the history of Friends' books of discipline, signed 'P.P.'], *The Friend*, vol. 117, 20 November 1959, p. 1371.

'"Meetings settled, discontinued or united". A summary of reports to London Yearly Meeting, 1834-1890', *Journal of Friends Historical Society*, vol. 49, no. 2, Spring 1960, pp. 97-103.

'Appendix: Quaker and anti-Quaker writings, 1660-1665', in *The Beginnings of Nonconformity 1660-1665: a checklist*, edited by Geoffrey F.Nuttall (Dr. Williams's Library, 1960, duplicated typescript), ff.[90-128].

'Society of Friends records' [part of an article on Protestant Nonconformist records], *Archives*, vol. 5, no. 25, Lady Day 1961, pp. 11-12.

'A Quaker translation' [of the Bible, by Anthony Purver (1702-1777), unsigned], *The Wayfarer*, vol. 40, April 1961, p. 60.

'As it was?' [London Yearly Meeting as portrayed in 'The Quakers synod', a caricature, 1698, unsigned], *The Wayfarer*, vol. 40, May 1961, p. 76.

[An account of the library exhibition at London Yearly Meeting 1962, unsigned] *The Friend*, vol. 120, 8 June 1962, p. 724.

'London Yearly Meeting, 1962' [unsigned], *Friends Journal* (Philadelphia), vol. 6, 1 July 1962, pp. 275-76.

'Colchester Quakers' [review of *Colchester Quakers*, by Stanley H.G.Fitch (Colchester, Essex, 1962), signed 'EHM'], *The Friend*, vol. 120, 14 September 1962, pp. 1128-30.

'Standard-bearers in New England' [review of *The Standard of the Lord Lifted Up*, by Mary Hoxie Jones (Freeport, Maine, 1961), signed 'Antiquax'], *The Friend*, vol. 121, 25 January 1963, pp. 95-97.

'John L.Milligan' [(1881-1963): an obituary of Edward H.Milligan's father, prefaced 'A Friend writes . . .'], *The Friend*, vol. 121, 20 September 1963, p. 1086.

'An early mail robbery' [an account of Frederick Smith (1757-1823), signed 'Antiquax'], *The Friend*, vol. 121, 27 December 1963, p. 1533.

'"God the disturber"' [a letter to the editor, on Alec Lea's article of that title], *The Friend*, vol. 122, 20 March 1964, p. 358.

'Centenary of Luke Howard' [(1772-1864), signed 'Antiquax'], *The Friend*, vol. 122, 20 March 1964, pp. 338-39.

'Edith M.Sturge' [(1875-1964): an obituary, prefaced 'A Friend writes . . .'], *The Friend*, vol. 122, 6 November 1964, p. 1328.

'Family sketches of a hundred years ago [review of *Family Sketchbooks a Hundred Years Ago*, by E.Ellen Buxton, edited by E.R.C.Creighton (1964)], *The Friend*, vol. 122, 18 December 1964, p. 1536.

'Friends, Society of', *Encyclopaedia Britannica*, 1964, vol. 9, pp. 938-43.

'William Hope-Jones' [(1884-1965): an obituary, signed 'Y'], *The Friend*, vol. 123, 5 March 1965, pp. 258-59.

'An early Friend of Bishoprick' [Anthony Pearson (1628?-1665/6), signed 'Antiquax'], *The Friend*, vol. 123, 21 May 1965, pp. 589-90.

Report of Berks & Oxon Quarterly Meeting, 30 October 1965 [signed 'M'], *The Friend*, vol. 123, 5 November 1965, p. 1344.

Britannica on Quakerism [being a reprint of the article in *Encyclopaedia Britannica*, 1964], (Friends Home Service Committee, 1965). 28pp.

Report of Berks & Oxon Quarterly Meeting, 29 January 1966 [signed 'M'] *The Friend*, vol. 124, 18 February 1966, p. 208.

'A note on the authorship of *The case of our fellow-creatures* (1784)' by Patrick C.Lipscomb III and Edward C[*sic*].Milligan, *Quaker History* (Philadelphia), vol. 55, no. 1, Spring 1966, pp. 47-51.

Report of Berks & Oxon Quarterly Meeting, 30 April 1966 [signed 'M'], *The Friend*, vol. 124, 13 May 1966, p. 568.

'List of members' [a letter to the editor, on the use of Roman and Arabic numbers for the months], *The Friend*, vol. 124, 3 June 1966, p. 651.

'Olive Wyon' [(1881?-1966): an obituary, unsigned], *The Friend*, vol. 124, 2 September 1966, p. 1030.

Report of Berks & Oxon Quarterly Meeting, 29 October 1966 [signed 'M'], *The Friend*, vol. 124, 9 December 1966, pp. 1482, 1484.

Quakers [being a Dutch translation, with some additions, of *Britannica on Quakerism* (1965), The Hague?, Netherlands Yearly Meeting, 1966]. 32pp.

Report of Berks & Oxon General Meeting, 28 January 1967 [signed 'M'], *The Friend*, vol. 125, 10 February 1967, pp. 183-84.

'Quaker ministry 1691-1834: the waning and waxing of a "note of joyful triumph"' [review of *Quaker Ministry 1691-1834*, by Lucia K.Beamish (Oxford, 1967)], *The Friend*, vol. 125, 26 May 1967, pp. 635-37, with a correction, 2 June 1967, p. 663.

'Absolute or relative?' [a review of Berks & Oxon General Meeting, signed 'M'], *The Friend*, vol. 125, 16 June 1967, p. 753.

Report of Berks & Oxon General Meeting, 24 June 1967 [signed 'M'], *The Friend*, vol. 125, 21 July 1967, pp. 894-95.

'Baltimore's past and future' [review of *Quaker Records in Maryland* by Phebe R.Jacobsen (Annapolis, Maryland, 1966), signed 'Antiquax'], *The Friend*, vol. 125, 28 July 1967, p. 925.

'Easy commerce of old and new' [report of Berks & Oxon General Meeting, 28 October 1967, signed 'M'], *The Friend*, vol. 125, 10 November 1967, pp. 1408-09.

'Simplicity' [an account of Berks & Oxon General Meeting's consideration of the subject, signed 'M'], *The Friend*, vol. 126, 21 June 1968, p. 740.

'W.H.F.Alexander' [a letter requesting a photograph of WHFA, signed by Edward H.Milligan as librarian], *The Friend*, vol. 126, 21 June 1968, p. 754.

'"... Rightly dividing the word of truth": *Church Government* revision' [signed 'Antiquax'], *The Friend*, vol. 126, 5 July 1968, pp. 797-98.

'Meeting houses, past and present' [a letter to the editor, on Friends' meeting openly and not in secret in the seventeenth century], by Edward H.Milligan and Richenda C.Scott, *The Friend*, vol. 126, 30 August 1968, pp. 1091-92.

The Past is Prologue: 100 Years of Quaker Overseas Work 1868-1968 [by Edward H.Milligan.] (Friends Service Council, 1968). 64pp.

'All manner of human frailty. [Abridged from] a talk given at the meeting of overseers during [London] Yearly Meeting 1969', *Friends Quarterly*, vol. 16, no. 9, January 1970, pp. 443-57.

'"Glorious Devon"' and 'Friends in the south west' [unsigned], and 'Getting to know one another' [signed 'Antiquax', being part of the introduction to] London Yearly Meeting *Proceedings*, 1970, pp. 11-19.

'The religious meaning of marriage: the Quakers' [including editorial additions], *Brides and Setting Up Home*, vol. 13, no. 2, Spring 1970, pp. 68-69.

'"Too deep for tears": Wordsworth and the faculty of imagination', *The Friend*, vol. 128, 3 April 1970, pp. 381-83.

'George Newman centenary' [an account of a meeting held by the Society for the Social History of Medicine to commemorate the birth of Sir George Newman (1870-1948), unsigned], *The Friend*, vol. 128, 16 October 1970, p. 1293.

'Archivists at Friends House' [an account of a visit to the library by members of the south-east region of the Society of Archivists, unsigned], *The Friend*, vol. 128, 11 December 1970, p. 1476.

'999' [a letter to the editor on the numbering of sections in *Church Government* (1968), signed 'Antiquax'], *The Friend*, vol. 129, 8 January 1971, p. 45.

'George Newman [1870-1948]—centenary reflections', *Friends Quarterly*, vol. 17, no. 1, January 1971, pp. 28-33.

'Down to earth Quakerism' [review of *The Minute Book of the Men's Meeting of the Society of Friends in Bristol, 1667-1686*, edited by Russell S.Mortimer (Bristol, 1971)], *The Friend*, vol. 129, 28 May 1971, pp. 625-26.

'Children's day at Friends House' [signed 'M'], *The Friend*, vol. 129, 6 August 1971, p. 948.

'Peter Scott' [(1890-1972): an obituary], *Friends Quarterly*, vol. 17, no. 6, April 1972, pp. 242-43.

'Questions to Friends' [letter to the editor on the misreporting of Friends], *The Friend*, vol. 131, 10 August 1973, p. 961.

'Two of a sort' [the tercentenary of the Library of London Yearly Meeting], *The Friend*, vol. 131, 14 September 1973, pp. 1097-99.

'Henry J.Cadbury: the man and the teacher' [a ninetieth birthday tribute], *Friends Quarterly*, vol. 18, no. 4, October 1973, pp. 152-53.

'Titles and functions of meetings', in *Sources for Nonconformist Genealogy and Family History* (National Index of Parish Registers, vol. 2), by D.J.Steel (1973), pp. 611-21.

'Henry J.Cadbury' [(1883-1974): an obituary], *Friends Quarterly*, vol. 19, no. 1, January 1975, pp. 2-3.

'The loquacious Bushell' [a letter to the editor on 'Bushell's case', 1670, signed 'Antiquax'], *The Friend*, vol. 133, 15 August 1975, p. 934.

'Rosamund Wallis' [(1892-1976): an obituary], *The Friend*, vol. 134, 16 April 1976, p. 435.

'Douglas Millard' [(1903-1976): an obituary], by Dermot O'C.Grubb and Edward H.Milligan, *The Friend*, vol. 134, 30 April 1976, p. 503.

'Met pursuant to adjournment' [on London Yearly Meeting's ceasing to use the term at the beginning of its sessions], *Quaker Monthly*, vol. 55, September 1976, pp. 164-65.

'Why we come to meeting' [a letter to the editor on the misreporting of Friends], *The Friend*, vol. 135, 25 March 1977, p. 344.

'Margaret Backhouse' [(1887-1977): an obituary], *The Friend*, vol. 135, 15 April 1977, pp. 423-24.

'Is all well?' [The usefulness of administrative queries on orderly business methods and the preservation of Friends' records, signed 'Custos'], *The Friend*, vol. 135, 26 August 1977, pp. 997-98.

'A tribute to Geoffrey Nuttall' [review of *Reformation, Conformity and Dissent: Essays in Honour of Geoffrey Nuttall*, edited by R.Buick Knox (1977)], *The Friend*, vol. 136, 3 March 1978, p. 251.

'First World War records' [a letter to the editor on the deposit of papers relating to conscientious objectors, signed by Edward H.Milligan as librarian], *The Friend*, vol. 136, 30 June 1978, p. 805.

'Amy E.Wallis' [(1886-1978): an obituary], *The Friend*, vol. 136, 14 July 1978, pp. 865-66.

'News from darkest Berks' [an appeal for East Garston meeting house], *The Friend*, vol. 136, 21 July 1978, pp. 889-90.

'Thanks for eleven years' [a tribute to Richenda C.Scott, retiring editor], *Friends Quarterly*, vol. 20, no. 7, July 1978, p. 319.

'Quaker peace witness' [review of *Quaker Peace Work on Merseyside*, by M.Muriel Shearer (Southport, Merseyside, 1979)], *The Friend*, vol. 137, 14 September 1979, p. 1146.

'Wilfrid Littleboy' [(1885-1979): an obituary by L.Hugh Doncaster and Edward H.Milligan], *The Friend*, vol. 137, 28 September and 5 October 1979, pp. 1195-97 and 1229-30.

'Evening reading' [address delivered at the Easter Gathering 1979, Ackworth School, West Yorkshire], Ackworth School Old Scholars Association, *Annual Report*, no. 98, 1979, pp. 38-40.

So Numerous a Family. 1779-1979: 200 Years of Quaker Education at Ackworth (Ackworth, West Yorkshire, 1979). ['The School Committee has entrusted the preparation of the text and the illustrations to Elfrida Vipont Foulds and Edward Milligan.'] 60pp.

Unity in the Spirit: Quakers and the Ecumenical Pilgrimage. [Drafted by Edward H.Milligan] (Quaker Home Service, for the Committee on Christian Relationships, 1979.) 25pp.

'Did punctuality matter?' [Review of *The Minute Book of the Men's Meeting of the Society of Friends in Bristol, 1686-1704*, edited by Russell S.Mortimer (Bristol, 1977)], *The Friend*, vol. 138, 18 April 1980, pp. 471-72.

'Unchronicled Barchester—and a few recent chronicles of our local meetings', *Friends Quarterly*, vol. 22, no. 3, July 1980, pp. 325-34.

'The light of Asia' [review of *Quakers in India*, by Marjorie Sykes (1980)], *Friends World News*, no. 115, Autumn 1980, pp.11-12.

'Pennsylvania's important year' [the tercentenary of the granting of the charter of Pennsylvania to William Penn], *The Friend*, vol. 139, 6 March 1981, p. 276.

'Philadelphia through the eyes of country Friends' [review of *Quaker Roots—the Story of Western Quarterly Meeting of Philadelphia Yearly Meeting* (Kennett Square, Pennsylvania, 1980), *The Friend*, vol. 139, 25 September 1981, p. 1222.

'Margaret Crook' [(1890-1982): an obituary], *The Friend*, vol. 140, 29 January 1982, p. 104.

'Beatrice Saxon Snell [(1900-1982): an obituary], *The Friend*, vol. 140, 5 February 1982, pp. 139-40.

'"To Friends everywhere." Reflections on the epistle in the life of London Yearly Meeting', *Friends Quarterly*, vol. 22, no. 11, July 1982, pp. 724-36.

'Richard Stagg' [(1926-1982): an obituary], *The Friend*, vol. 140, 3 December 1982, pp. 1527-28.

'Frieda Bacon' [(1897-1983): an obituary], *The Friend*, vol. 141, 13 May 1983, p. 590.

My Ancestors Were Quakers. How Can I Find Out More About Them? By Edward H.Milligan and Malcolm J.Thomas (Society of Genealogists, 1984). [iv]+ii+37pp.

'George W.Edwards' [(1892-1983): an obituary], *The Friend*, vol. 142, 27 January 1984, pp. 105-06.

'"In reason's ear": some Quaker and Anglican perplexities', *Friends Quarterly*, vol. 23, no. 8, October 1984, pp. 389-96.

Margaret Fell: Mother of Quakerism, by Isabel Ross [2nd edition, edited and with a 'note to the 1984 edition' by Edward H.Milligan and Malcolm J.Thomas] (York: William Sessions Book Trust, 1984). xviii+422pp.

SUBSCRIBERS

Sybil K.Abbott
Ackworth Old Scholars Association
Mary & Ted Adley
Betsy & William Aitken
Michael & Eleanor Aitken
Peter & Beth Allen
Richard Allen
Edrey & Stephen Allott
Trevor & Jean Allcock
Anne & William Ashmore
Ashton-on-Mersey PM Library
May (Burgess) Avery &
   Robert G.Avery

Toby Bainton
John Banks
D.M.Cecil Barker
Dudley J.Barlow
Alfred & Margaret Bayes
Sidney Beck
Roger A.Bellingham
Birmingham Bull Street PM
   Library
Mary Blaschko
Michael J.M. & Marjorie Bliss
Bernard W.Blunsom
Brian F.Bone
Marcella Bowes
Barbara A.Bowman
Bertha L.Bracey

Bradford PM Library
M.Millior Braithwaite
Brian Bridge
Richard K.Brown
Jim & Eleanor Brunton
Rosemary Butler

Jack & Tessa Cadbury
Venetia Caine
Anne Carey
Reg Carr
J.Norman Cartwright
E.Ann Castle
Rosemarie Cawson
Ann Chase
Cheshire MM
Robert Clark & Susan Costello
Vivian C.Clark
Chris & Karen Coffin
Kathleen M.Cooper
Allen H.Cullum
Ann Cuming

Frances F.Dagnell
Jonathan Dale
Margaret Dale
Michael S.Darby
Darlington PM Library
Hilda M.Davies
Christine & Robin Davis

Beth Dearden
Michael R.Delf
Christopher Denman
Jessie E.Dicks
L.Hugh & L.Cecilia Doncaster
Thelma Done
Tabitha Driver

Angus W.Earnshaw
Pamela & Peter J.Eccles
Frank A.Edmunds
C.Leonard Elliott
Dorothy M.R.Ellis
John Endersby
Epsom PM Library
David Eversley

Ruth Mary Fawell
Walter Fearnley
David & Jill Firth
Kenneth & Olive Ford
Muriel & Bill Frank
William & Nancy Fraser
Mary W.Fulford

Irene M.Gay
Tony & Eirene Gilpin
Bernard Gooch
Ronald & Maggie Goodrich
Lucy M.Gorman
Judith Baresel Graham
Betty C.Gray
David & Margaret Gray
Dermot & Jane Grubb
Martyn Grubb
Mollie E.Grubb
Guildford PM Library
Mary Guillemard

Bernard Hadley
Clifford Haigh
Jolyon Hall

Barbara Halliburton
John & Susan Hartshorne
John Hawkins
Jack & Florence Haworth
Mary Hayman
L.Theodora Headley
Bernt Heid
Robert J.P.Hewison
Jane Heydecker
Paul & Catherine Hickinbotham
Gerald A.J.Hodgett
Brigit Hodgkin
Robin & Elizabeth Hodgkin
Sheila & Lawrence Holderness
Judith J.Holding
Christopher J.Holdsworth
R.Eric Holttum
Gillian E.Hopkins
John Horsley
Lily Howe
Audrey Hughes
Michael & Margaret Hughes
Elizabeth & Stanley Hunt
Michael J.Hutchinson

Irene Jacoby
Constance Jarrett
Roy & Nell Jarvis
David S.Jeffrey
Jo & Bernice Joachim
Mary & Stanley Jones
Sally Juniper

Stephen & Eileen Kemp
Nancy Kershaw & A.Lois Bulley
Josiah Knight
Margaret & Charles Kohler

A.Christopher Lake
David Lanham
A.Margaret Laurie
Robert J.Leach

172

Arnold J.Leather
Betty & Michael Lee
Doris & Douglas Lee
Marjorie H.Lee
Joan Legelli
Winifred E.Lewis
Albert F.Lindley
Muriel A.K.Lindsay
Brian & Diane Livesey
John Lockett
Rowena Loverance

Godfrey & Dorothy Mace
Duncan Macfarlane & Derek
  Watts
Trevor Macpherson
Marjorie MacRae
Dorothy Manasseh
Manchester PM Library
Mary Mander
Marion C.Mansergh
Doris S.Martin
Mary C.Martin
Philip L.Martin
Eva M.Maw
Annemarie McAllister
Joseph McGarraghy
Myrtle McTear
Audrey Mitchell
David & Madeline Mitchell
Jean & Russell Mortimer
Margaret Morton
W.T. & S.S. Morton
Harold Myers

Richard E.Naish
Desmond & Joyce Neill
John L.Nickalls
Marian G.Noble
E.M.North

Elsie & Arthur G.Olver

E.Kelvin Osborn

J.H.P.Pafford
Damaris Parker-Rhodes
Roy Payne
Gay Pembroke
John H.Pierse
Harry W.Polley
Muriel Poulter
James Priestman
John Punshon
Muriel Putz

H.A.Farrand Radley
Joyce D.Radley
Myrtle & Philip Radley
Arthur Raistrick
Ted Randall
Chas Raws
Reading PM Library
Harold Reed
Reigate PM Library
Antony & Johanne Reynolds
Robert Rigby
Peter F.H.Robson
Margery H.R.Routledge
Margaret Rowe
Mary Rowlands
Elizabeth M.Rowntree
Martin & Mary Rowntree
Richard S. & Mary P.Rowntree

Douglas Sanders
Richard Schardt
Peter & Muriel Seaby
R.Martin Seddon
E.Margaret & William K.Sessions
Joseph B. & Janet Sewell
John Shackleton
Cecil W.Sharman
M.Muriel Shearer
Sibford School Library

Nicholas A.Sims
Gil Skidmore
Julius Smit & Peter Norris
Noel Smith
Marjorie & Raymond South
Christine M.Spray
Harry & Muriel Stevens
Michael B.Stevens
Sylvia Stevens
R.Margaret Stone
Ann & Kurt Strauss
Roger & Hilda Sturge
Margaret E.Sullivan
Mary S.Sutherland
Grace Sutton
Walter F.Sweatman
Alan Swerdlow

Polly Tatum
Irene Taylor
S.John Teague
Irene Tester
Geraldine Theobald
Pearson Thistlethwaite
Kevin B.Thompson
Mary Tillett
Robert J.N.Tod
Eric S.Tucker

Erica Vere

Ben Vincent
E.Margaret Vokes

Graham & Vi Walker
Kathleen & Ronald Walker
Ruth M.Wall
John Ward
Stella & Geoffrey Ward
Emlyn Warren
Joshua Watts
Charles Webb-Fowler
Richard & Dorothy Webster
Jane Wedmore
Ronald Weitzman
Welwyn Garden City PM Library
Margaret West
Edna H.White
Vernon White
Edwin A.Whiting
Joan & Clifford Wicken
Helen Widdowson
Stephen Wilson
Patrick & Marion Winchester
Denys E.Wingfield
Eric S.Wood
Linda & Simon Wood
Woodbrooke Library
Jack & Carrie Wrightson

Christina Yates

The production of this book owes much to the care and generosity of Headley Brothers in printing it. Design and lay-out have been the responsibility of Jeremy Greenwood. The cover design is by John Blamires. One copy has been specially bound for Edward H.Milligan by Vanessa Marshall with materials provided by Val Ferguson.

CONTRIBUTORS

CHRIS BARBER Chairman of Social Responsibility Council, 1970-72; Clerk of Quaker Social Responsibility and Education, 1979-81; Henley-on-Thames Meeting

MELANIE BARBER Clerk of Library Committee; editor of *Friends Quarterly*, 1980-85; Brighton Meeting

DAVID BLAMIRES Member of Library Committee and Quaker Home Service; author of *A History of Quakerism in Liversedge and Scholes;* Manchester Meeting

THOMAS R.BODINE Clerk of New England Yearly Meeting, 1962-67; Clerk of Friends United Meeting, Richmond, Indiana, 1972-75; Hartford, Connecticut, Meeting

GEOFFREY BOWES Recording Clerk of London Yearly Meeting; Lewes Meeting

DAVID M.BUTLER Author of *Quaker Meeting Houses in the Lake Counties;* Kendal Meeting

KENNETH L.CARROLL Author of *John Perrot, Early Quaker Schismatic;* regular visitor to England and Ireland over twenty-five years; Dallas, Texas, Meeting

JO FARROW General Secretary of Quaker Home Service; Littlehampton Meeting

ELFRIDA VIPONT FOULDS Clerk of Meeting for Sufferings, 1969-74; author of some fifty books including *Colin Writes to Friends House* and *The Story of Quakerism;* contributor to *Mount Street 1830-1930;* Yealand Meeting

ORMEROD GREENWOOD Author of *Quaker Encounters*, 3 vols.; Swarthmore Lecturer 1978 with *Signs of Life: Art and Religious Experience;* Eastbourne Meeting

HOWARD F.GREGG Member of Library Committee; Wandsworth Meeting

DAVID J.HALL Member of Library Committee; Cambridge Oast House Meeting

HOPE HEWISON Secretary of Friends Community Relations Committee, 1971-74; author of *The Quakers;* Westminster Meeting

ALEX KERR Clerk of Berks & Oxon General Meeting; Faringdon Meeting

JON NORTH Member of Library staff, 1973-77; Secretary of Premises and Services Committee, Friends House, 1977-83; Fritchley Meeting

JANET SCOTT Swarthmore Lecturer 1980 with *What Canst Thou Say? Towards a Quaker Theology;* Sevenoaks Meeting

MALCOLM J.THOMAS Member of Library staff; Librarian in succession to Edward H.Milligan

LESLEY WEBSTER Member of Library staff, 1972-78; Croydon Meeting

ARTHUR J.WHITE Recording Clerk of London Yearly Meeting, 1966-78; Sutton Meeting

ROGER C.WILSON General Secretary of Friends Relief Service, 1940-45; Swarthmore Lecturer 1949 with *Authority, Leadership and Concern;* Clerk of London Yearly Meeting, 1975-77; Yealand Meeting

JOHN BLAMIRES Poster designer and cover designer for very many Quaker publications; Bradford Meeting

VAL FERGUSON Associate Secretary of Friends World Committee for Consultation; Friends House Meeting

JEREMY GREENWOOD Assistant Clerk of London Yearly Meeting, 1983-84; typographic designer; Liverpool Meeting

HEADLEY BROTHERS The Invicta Press, Ashford, Kent, printers of *The Friend*, *Friends Quarterly* and very many London Yearly Meeting documents and publications

VANESSA MARSHALL Bookbinder; Friends House Meeting